ANGEL ON MY SHOULDER

JOHN REYNOLDS

"The days are long gone when I could beat you in a half marathon. Since then, you have amazed us all with your first major charity run of 110 miles non-stop, then 140 with a sprint finish, then a mere 300 from Land's End to Bath, and finally (but not so finally) the 426 over seven days. There are so many memories of these and many more trips, especially things like the time you went to sleep standing up having your neck massaged by Margaret! It's been an honour and a pleasure, even with the pain. You used to be the quiet man, but your achievements tell the story as loud as anything."
Bob Powell

"Well done John! The things I've seen you do over the years if we believe we can reach our goals. Thank you."
Roger Sperring

"You are simply the best! You have inspired, challenged and encouraged so many with your running enthusiasm. The running family you have grown is testament to the values you hold. Acceptance of all, determination, support and above all else give it a go – no one is ever left behind or excluded and that is why so many achieve what they thought was impossible. Thank you."
Lucy Jefferyes

"You have inspired, and continue to inspire so many John – and the support you and Jo give is obvious to all."
Sue Tucker

"You know this whole magnificent bunch is entirely down to you and your unlimited enthusiasm for all people achieving their potential. From plodders to crazy nutters, you've built one hell of an extended family."
Rich Morley

"So proud of all you've achieved John and it's been a privilege to have accompanied you on some of your adventures. An absolute honour to know you and the inspiration that you are for the local running communities. Always a little further."
Baz Eggy

"John Reynolds is an absolute inspiration to us all. His enthusiasm for life in real adversity, his sheer grit and determination has always amazed me - he's raised incredible amounts for charities and smashed out so many miles utterly astounding for someone who had to learn to walk again. Above all, he's one of the nicest people you'd ever wish to meet - and he'll tell you some brilliant stories over a pint of Guinness (or two!). John Reynolds - legend."
Becky Brooks

This book is dedicated to
Steve and Phil
(Wilf and Sarge)

You were my family and best friends,
taken far too early.

You have always been,
and will continue to be, my inspiration

Bristol Books CIC, The Courtyard, Wraxall,
Wraxall Hill, Bristol, BS48 1NA

Angel On My Shoulder
written by John Reynolds

Published by Bristol Books 2022

ISBN: 9781909446328

Design: Joe Burt

A CIP record for this book is available from the British Library.

To all the Staff at
C.HSW.

Many thanks for all the amazing
work you do.

Best Wishes
John Reynolds.

CONTENTS

"As Co-Founder and Chief Executive of CHSW I want to thank the readers of John's book for joining with us to ensure we can continue to be there for families when they need us most."

Eddie Farwell

INTRODUCTION

Life can take you in so many different directions – not always as you had planned. Sometimes the journey may seem impossible, but I have found that if you search hard enough, there is always a positive outcome to be made from every situation. That the impossible can become possible. If you grasp hold of, and believe in, the slightest glimmer of hope.

John Reynolds

ACHIEVING THE IMPOSSIBLE

Propped with my back firmly resting against an old stone wall in my cottage, I peacefully lay on the wooden floor with my legs casually spread out before me.

I remember the moment more vividly than any other because, at the time, I didn't realise or have a clue as to how much it would change my life forever.

It was Christmas Day 2004 and the morning had quietly slipped away without me noticing. I was in my own little world, surrounded by a million and one different thoughts, as the hours passed by.

My thoughts were of images of everyone celebrating Christmas together; brightly lit rooms full of laughter, the sharing of presents, probably the only quiet times would be the afternoon naps following a long delicious dinner.

As evening approached, I reached over and casually read the label on the bottle of whiskey that I had nearby. I must have seen this label hundreds of times before, but on this occasion I chose to read it purely out of a form of distraction. As the whiskey left the bottle – filling the room with its strong aroma and distinct glugging noise – my faithful springer spaniel Scooby raised his ears and eyes towards me as if for reassurance that everything would be okay.

I adjusted my sitting position to try and get comfortable on the hard floor as Scooby reassuringly lay with his head across my legs, firmly pressing downwards as if to stop me from going anywhere.

As darkness quickly engulfed us we must have portrayed a right sorrowful pair of casualties. Scooby at the age of just 12 weeks had broken his leg by taking a huge tumble while ambitiously chasing a very fit pair of rabbits across a rough field, while I was recovering from radiotherapy after treatment to cure a really aggressive thyroid condition.

Due to my treatment I was advised not to visit other people, especially young children, for at least a ten day period due to the exposure of radiation, and Scooby was advised to have complete rest while his leg was encased in a solid cast of plaster.

I was temporarily distracted from deep within my thoughts by the sound of Scooby lapping up his Christmas portion of whiskey from the tumbler conveniently positioned by his side.

Half a glass later he raised his head to look directly into my face as if to question why I hadn't yet drank any. Then with his huge fluffy ears sliding forward to cover his eyes he promptly sneezed, showering me in the remnants, which for the next few minutes I continued to find and wipe away with a quick swipe of the arm.

To release the room from darkness and feel some sense of accomplishment from all the inactivity, I lit the fire and resumed my position back on the floor with Scooby. Moments later the silence was broken by my faithful companion's incessant snoring – at least he was comfortable and relaxed despite his injury, which to me was the most important thing that day.

At the age of 42 and having lived a reasonably healthy lifestyle – apart from the occasional all night long parties, top shelf challenges in the local pub and devouring meals that probably could have fed 10 people in a single serving – I always thought that I was in a pretty fit condition.

So when I dramatically started to lose weight and feel tired – despite consuming a trolley load of groceries – I began to suspect something was wrong. At first I tried to convince myself that my tiredness was caused by the amount of energy used to eat all this food each day but common sense soon prevailed and with pounds of weight still being lost I decided to make a very rare visit to my local GP.

After some trial blood tests and thoroughly convincing myself that nothing was wrong, my confidence was taken aside when I received a referral to quickly see a specialist in my nearest hospital a few days later.

I thought I'd always been fit and healthy and with Christmas not far away presumed it couldn't be serious. I confidently marched into the consultant's room where I was promptly told that I needed to receive medical attention almost immediately, otherwise my future looked pretty doubtful.

Just 12 days later I was receiving radiotherapy for a severe thyroid condition that was out of control and dissolving my body, along with all the extra food I was consuming. From previously having nothing wrong with myself – apart from the odd cold – to this predicament was a real shock and seriously worrying at the time.

While receiving treatment in hospital I couldn't believe how young some of the children were, who were also receiving radiotherapy. My thoughts rapidly changed from feeling sorry for myself and wondering why this was happening to me, to having the upmost respect for all these youngsters and their families. All the children – despite in some cases going through such severe medical treatment – were still resilient, smiling and happy, which made me look again at my own situation. I suddenly felt as though I had been so selfish, feeling sorry for myself and worrying about what was going to happen to me. Here I was having had 42 healthy years of life and enjoyment, yet these little ones had only experienced in some cases four or five years of their lives and had a very uncertain future ahead of them. It was then that I vowed to myself that if I could make a recovery and be fit enough to raise some funds for children's charities then that would be my main priority.

As the month of January slowly passed the burning sensation in my throat decreased and I felt a lot more comfortable. I began to think how I could start raising money for the children and their families.

I returned to work after the Christmas break and felt reasonably comfortable health-wise in my job as a civil engineer. It could be very physically demanding at times but I always enjoyed the various new and interesting building projects.

But by February I noticed that various everyday tasks were taking slightly longer than normal to accomplish, along with feeling an overwhelming sense of tiredness. The easiest and simplest way that I can explain the condition to others was that it was like I had a handbrake permanently in the "on" position fitted to me.

Simple work tasks became harder to achieve until, one evening after work, the whole of my body seemed to shut down and every muscle became a source of pain.

The next morning, after an entire night of broken sleep, it became a real struggle with the excruciating pain to even put a pair of socks on, let alone venture to work.

After being diagnosed with having severe muscle spasms affecting my back, I received a prescription for morphine-based medication. The pain did then eventually ease, releasing me from what seemed like invisible chains that bound me almost motionless. But by taking the strong medication another problem was created which I'd never had the misfortune to experience before. I felt a horrible sense of not having any control over my actions, accompanied with a general feeling of drowsiness. I knew what I wanted to achieve each day but could never complete these tasks. This proved really frustrating and another form of self-entrapment.

After two days on the strong medication, I phoned my cousins, Steve and Phil, and invited them around to explain what was happening to my health and what my future plans were.

Steve and Phil were two of my cousins who were always on hand and very close to me; we had all grown up together on our Nan's dairy farm based in the picturesque Chew Valley, on grounds next to the lake.

Steve was two years older than me, and Phil was four years older, so I was the baby of the group and quickly learnt to grow up in order to achieve the same goals on their level. We were always there to support each other in times of need. Right from the moment we learnt to walk and find out the true meaning of mischievousness, we made our own adventures together, and we were often referred to as the "Last of the Summer Wine bunch" throughout our school years, with Steve (Wilf) being the character known as "Compo".

As I sat with Steve and Phil, and explained my situation and told them I no longer wanted to be on medication, the look on their faces was of major concern. Their reaction was to immediately disagree, as each frankly explained their reasons and concerns for my health. The one thing above all others that I thoroughly respected from both Steve and Phil throughout the years was their complete honesty – if they ever thought that something wasn't right then they would immediately tell me without any hesitation.

I listened to them as they told me why I should continue on full medication until both of them could say no more to convince me otherwise. However, it made no difference, I was sticking firmly with my decision and explained to them there was no way that I wanted to exist in a future dictated by really strong drugs where I had very little or no control.

The debate continued for some time until eventually they could see my decision was final and there was no way of convincing me otherwise. That evening I asked if they would take my medication away with them, otherwise I would dispose of it immediately. By taking it with them they soon realised if I did change my mind that they could always bring it back to me.

After countless remarks of "you just look after yourself" and "just give us a ring if you need anything" they disappeared into the night, shaking their heads in dismay, taking my poison (as I referred to it) with them.

Several times during the night I awoke on the sofa. Each time I was overwhelmed by a continuous blanket of pain and found it easier to remain as still as possible until the time came that I had to move for a specific reason. I found the sofa to be the most comfortable place to sleep as I didn't want to risk climbing up and down the steep staircase in the cottage.

Every time I rose to my feet it was complete agony with tears quickly forming in my eyes hampering my vision as I reached out for support, holding onto the dining room door where I could rest for a moment before continuing my journey across the rest of the house.

Thoughts kept entering my mind like mini explosions. Perhaps Steve and Phil were right? Had I been too hasty in my decision? Perhaps if I had kept going on the medication then most of the pain that I was now experiencing would no longer be with me!

Throughout the night my thoughts were tormenting me. It felt as if I had a demon sitting firmly on one shoulder debating all the reasons for keeping the medication, and an angel sitting on the other shoulder reassuring me that I had made the right decision and highlighting all the good things that would come from this.

I was eventually distracted by the fact that it was now daylight outside and I could see the first few golden rays of sunlight as they pierced through the cottage windows, filling me with a positive and warm sense of satisfaction that things would be okay. I watched the sun in full admiration as it gently rose into the fresh blue sky, now leaving the dark hills from where it had risen far below.

With the physical condition that I was now in, it was impossible to go back to work and carry out everyday duties. I was more of a liability than anything else, especially to my work colleagues, so I had to focus on different jobs and things of interest around the house.

After writing a list of things to concentrate on completing, I decided that it was my goal for the day to plant up some flower seeds in the greenhouse so that they would be at the correct stage of growth for replanting later in the summer months.

On leaving the house I had no idea how painful and hard the

simple task of walking up the garden to reach the greenhouse could be; a walk that I'd presviously taken for granted and performed hundreds of times without ever giving a second thought to.

It took me well over an hour to shuffle the 60-metre journey, while taking frequent rests, supporting myself on walls, fences and garden gates until I eventually arrived at the greenhouse.

Even the simplest of tasks, like sliding the door open, was excruciating and felt like I was trying to move a mountain.

Pulling an old stool out from under the bench I managed to settle down and start sowing the seeds that would bring my garden into colour. I dreamt of how good it would be to have a cup of tea, but that was certainly out of the question at this point in time.

Every simple task I undertook – like reaching out for fresh compost or a stack of pots – seemed to fail. The pain was excruciating and I had to override it in order to succeed at what I was doing.

As I made my perilous journey back down the garden to the house I spotted one of my neighbours. Each time we passed I waved out, pretending I was busy doing a job, instead of the reality that I was actually stopping just to recover from just walking.

Once back in my house I could relax again, sat with a warm cup of tea filling both hands. I had a smile for the first time in weeks as I reflected on how I had set myself a goal and successfully achieved it. I now had a strong sense of determination that I could achieve my goals without medication and felt I had a good future waiting ahead of me again.

Bursting with a brand new sense of confidence which seemed to override any pain, I phoned my cousins to enthusiastically explain what I had achieved and more importantly tell them, much to their relief, that I was okay.

STARTING LINE

Each new day I gave myself the goal of being able to walk further than the previous day. I was determined there would be no excuses at all, I wasn't going to skip a single day. I had to build back my strength so that I could be the same person that I was a few months earlier.

Two weeks later I felt confident enough to return back to work, which gave me a great confidence boost and reassured me that I was on the path track to recovery. Although I found my job hard at times, physically it was a great distraction, especially with the constant variety of tasks and new locations to travel to.

I had another appointment with the specialist at the hospital about my treatment and how things were progressing. They seemed to think that the seizures I was experiencing were caused by a waste product from the radiotherapy collecting in the muscle tissues.

By this time, I could now walk a reasonable distance and played down the seizures as I didn't want to go back on the recommended medication that I had experienced before.

One month on after my first walk up to the greenhouse without medication, I managed to walk a whole mile. For me this was a huge achievement and one that I seriously thought would be impossible to accomplish beforehand.

That evening I celebrated with my two cousins who were so relieved and finally believed in what I was trying to do.

All the time while I was pursuing each new goal, I kept thinking of all the children and their families that I had met during my treatment in hospital and of the ways in which I might be able to raise money and awareness for them. It was then that I heard from a friend who was taking part in the Midsomer Norton half marathon in June. This immediately gave me the idea that perhaps I could also cover the 13-mile circuit to raise some sponsorship money.

For the next few days I couldn't relinquish this thought from my mind. Several times I simply dismissed it as being ridiculous and miles too far for somebody like myself to even contemplate doing. But with each refusal that I gave myself there seemed to be a faint glimmer of hope, a spark that simply would not go away, whatever excuses I made, and beckoned me on to do this event. After a week of deliberation, I finally made the decision to enter the race and give myself just three months to train. Enough time to get from the one mile that I had just achieved, to the enormous 13-mile goal.

The challenge seemed impossible. But the excitement of thinking I could be that person who could complete a half marathon was enough to get me focused and training harder than I had ever done before. My aim was to add a mile every week on top of the mile that had just taken me a month to achieve.

By now Scooby had just had his plaster removed, and the operation where he'd had steel plates inserted into his leg had been a complete success. Like me he was now really keen to expand his distance while out walking.

Taking Scooby out with me in the evenings to achieve our new daily targets was a great help. I would talk to him about everything and anything while we were covering the miles. He would tilt his head and look directly at me in acknowledgement, as though he understood every word spoken.

My days were becoming more and more active, which was good, because the only times I really felt any pain from the muscle seizures was when I was resting for a significant length of time. During longer intervals of rest I would start to ache all over and every joint from head to foot would feel a dull pain at first, which soon got progressively worse. Night times especially proved to be the worst, with the greatest amount of discomfort leading to broken sleep. Each time I was woken by the pain – which could be three or four times a night – I would have to get out of bed and slowly walk around until, thankfully, it receded and I could feel reasonably comfortable again.

While feeling so tired in the middle of the night I would often curse no end to think of myself in this predicament, but then felt angry with myself at being so selfish. I was lucky enough to be able to walk the pain out of my body, while so many other people who I had seen in hospital didn't have that choice, and I was still free from the medication.

With all the exercise and walking longer distances, plus the dreaded night time experiences, there became a new problem. Every time I rested I risked not only the annoying seizures returning but also an overwhelming sense of tiredness. The continuous battle demanded more and more strength from my poor body, both physically and psychologically. At times during these breaks I would find myself falling asleep for several minutes without warning.

At one point, while sat on an old tree stump in a field chatting merrily to my cousin Steve, I fell asleep mid-conversation, with a cup of coffee in hand. Apparently, I woke up quite a few minutes later being told by him how arrogant I was to fall asleep during his conversation. He scornfully told me that I should "get to bed earlier, and by the way, that coffee I made you is now all over the floor!".

On another occasion, sat in the van in the village of Chew Stoke, I was filling in a works report form while Steve was looking for directions to get to the next venue. When I woke up still writing, I hadn't realised we'd travelled 15 miles to the centre of Cheddar, where I carried on the same conversation. Steve's explanation to me was "it was as though someone had recorded a conversation, paused it halfway through, and then continued to play it again half an hour later".

This was becoming a real worry to me, as well as embarrassing because it was happening in front of anyone whenever I decided to have a quick sit down or break. From then on I got Steve to wake me immediately, which he got great satisfaction from doing, by either giving me a good prod with his elbow or by splashing cold water over my face.

As the weeks seemed to go faster and faster approaching the half marathon, the training for both Scooby and myself seemed to be on schedule. My distance was now approaching eight miles – most of which I covered by a fast walking pace which I felt really pleased with. I can remember thinking to myself this was further than I had ever run before, and that most of the people entering the half marathon must be about the same speed as myself – after all, I now considered myself as reasonably fit!

It was on a Friday evening, while I was chilling out at home after finishing work and browsing a local free paper to discover the latest scandal to hit our region, when I came across an advert promoting a new sports club on the outskirts of Bath. They were holding an 80's music night that evening. After several minutes of deliberation and a pint of tea later I phoned Steve to see if he had anything planned for the evening. Seeing that we could both get in free of charge, so long as we presented the advert from the paper – and on the condition that they sold Guinness – he was up for it.

An hour later we were on our way into Bath. Driving into the club's large car park we couldn't help but notice how full it was. On entering the club I handed the creased and tatty looking advert that I had ripped out of the paper over to two stocky looking but well dressed gentlemen. Without exchanging words they eyed us up and down then gave a sharp tilt of the head, which we presumed gave us permission to enter.

On approaching the bar – much to my relief – I could see Guinness displayed amongst the illuminated beer pumps, which meant that Steve would be happy having his favourite fuel on tap.

As the evening progressed the dancefloor filled with more and more people. With this number of people dancing I felt I could easily join in with them, and considered myself pretty cool until I saw my reflection in a huge glass panel at the end of the bar. Suddenly I lost all confidence, became self-conscious, and then tried to correct my movements by observing others around me. Deciding that this was a mistake, I found it easier to ignore the mirror and do my own thing; besides, John Travolta didn't come from Somerset!

Every now and then Steve would appear from nowhere to join me on the dancefloor, then as quickly as he came he would vanish back to the safety of a bar stool next to the Guinness pump. From there he could casually and contentedly watch the world go about its business, Guinness held firmly in hand giving him the confidence to chat away to complete strangers.

On one particular occasion he was approached by three ladies who all broke out into a fit of giggles while dancing around him. Little did he know that it was me who had set him up! Looking over and seeing him move to the music as the trio approached the dancefloor I shouted to him "You've polished your love dome again haven't you?". This was the nick-name I gave his shiny head which was now fully absent of hair. In reply he gave a quick two-fingered gesture and solemn stare, as he danced away awkwardly trying to avoid his new friends, who relished in his torment. I knew deep down he secretly loved the banter though.

At the end of the evening, when all the slow songs started playing and couples were embracing each other romantically, we looked at each other, shrugged our shoulders and decided to make our way home via our favourite takeaway.

***

In the short weeks leading up to the Midsomer Norton half marathon the training was going well and I could now run more than eight miles, which I was really pleased with. But I must admit I did feel as though I had run 50 miles by the way my legs felt.

I kept telling myself that my progression from learning to walk my first mile back in March, to being able to achieve an eight-mile run in just three months, must surely be more than enough to get me through the 13 miles needed for the half marathon.

In June, walking down to Westfield trading estate to find the race start venue for the half marathon, I couldn't help but notice how much fitter a lot of the other runners seemed to be compared to myself. This was my first appearance at any race event since leaving school and was proving to be a real shock.

Peering down at my race number that I had so neatly pinned to my brilliant white running vest – purchased especially for the event – I suddenly noticed how much my belly protruded and quickly tried to pull in my stomach.

Above the sound of chatter we were called together by the event organiser who talked us through the race information. I managed to absorb only about half of this, as the rest was completely lost through my terrible lack of concentration as I worryingly analysed the other runners around me. My attention was then drawn to the bright sunshine as it began to break through the clouds to reveal a clear blue sky.

Standing amongst the line up of runners, all apprehensively waiting for the race to start, I looked around and realised that I didn't recognise a single person from the area. All the time that I had lived in Westfield I had spent my time either working away or endlessly renovating my cottage. I then spotted an old friend stood on the side line and promptly smiled at him and gave a half-hearted wave for self-assurance for what I was about to embark upon.

Ambling nervously around amongst all the other runners, I attempted to carry out a few warm up stretches, mainly to convince others around me that I was fully prepared and knew what I was doing, but in reality I didn't have a clue and just wanted to hide the severe doubts I was having.

Miles away in my own little world, I was suddenly brought back to reality by the sharp sound of an air-horn penetrating through the pre-race tension; this was it, the race had started!

For the first mile I felt really comfortable amongst the large number of competitors. I would happily smile at random spectators as they cheered us all along, shouting words of encouragement.

I suddenly realised how fast I had ran the first mile as my poor legs began to violently protest. I hadn't noticed this through looking at any modern sports watches or phone apps – I didn't own such equipment then. In all the excitement at the start of the run I had headed out with a totally false sense of confidence that I could keep up with the largest bunch of runners. I never considered how fast we were going as it felt good fun – after all I had plenty of training running my eight miles!

I watched as the main body of runners disappeared into the distance ahead of me. Some runners ran alongside me for brief periods, and greeted me with words of encouragement, while others were just focused on themselves and didn't alter their vision from the long road ahead. It felt like I was their target which they had to pass.

While going up the steep hill in Midsomer Norton, known locally as Silver Street, the sweat poured from my brow as never before, forming patterns on the hot tarmac around my tired feet. I tried in vain to hide the fact that I was melting like a snowman under the scalding sun which was now looming down unforgivingly.

I now realised that I had to walk the remainder of this never-ending hill, as I tried to comprehend how on earth anyone could ever run the full length of it. This distracted me temporarily from all the aches and pains in my body.

Finally, after reaching the top there was a water station where I found temporary relief from the thirst that now enraged my dry throat. A small group of people had formed just beyond the station, giving much needed encouragement, so I decided to make an effort and actually start running again. Struggling to swing one foot in front of the other, I managed a very slow and awkward jog. I kept thinking to myself as I peered into the distance "Where have all the runners disappeared to" as I envisaged some of them having already finished the race. Frantically I tried to focus on bringing some positivity back into my run.

From time to time a runner would slowly draw up alongside me, temporarily releasing a new hope in me as I tried to keep up with them. I tried to copy their leg movements and synchronise my pace with theirs, but all I could do was watch in sheer disappointment as another runner would fade away from me, swallowed up by the distant road ahead.

I would constantly keep looking behind me to reassure myself that there were still people out there running at a slower speed than me. I had to keep pushing forward to that finish line.

Counting down the mile markers became soul destroying. I tried to ignore them by looking away, then at the very last second glance back at them just to check and in a strange but tormented way reassure myself.

The marshals were really good; offering advice and reassuring us on the final miles that we didn't have much further to travel. The last few miles felt like ten, even with the amazing support given by both the crowds and runners who had returned back out on the circuit to encourage us.

Long gone were the issues that I had experienced earlier – like trying to hold my belly in to look like an Olympic athlete. I didn't care now if it was so big that it dragged along the floor as I entered the last mile of the run through quiet country lanes.

Then came the moment I had struggled so long for, the last few hundred metres. My legs were beginning to shake and buckle under both the excitement and the strain of the run.

On entering a sports field, I could now see the two bright posts of the finish line only a hundred metres ahead. All around me I could hear the much appreciated enthusiasm coming from both the spectators and marshals who guided me reassuringly across the finish line.

I painfully waddled through the taped funnel that led to more jubilant marshals, full of praise and encouragement, who handed me a much welcome drink along with a souvenir drinks bottle that I will always cherish.

Lost deep in my thoughts, I wondered how anybody could find enjoyment by putting themselves through so much pain. At that moment I thought I would never want to attempt anything like this again. I was then suddenly brought back to reality when somebody grabbed hold of me and gave me a huge bear hug before dropping me back on my feet as they began protesting how wet I had made them through all the sweat.

It was my two cousins, Phil and Steve, who had patiently waited to see me to cross the finish line.

"Did you jump in a pond on the way round?"

"What took you so long – we've been down the pub twice while waiting for you to come in."

They both stood there with a bottle of champagne and smiles that would light up the world, which instantly made me feel like the happiest and luckiest person alive.

PRIDE AND DETERMINATION

After completing the Midsomer Norton half marathon I felt really pleased that I had accomplished my personal goal while also raising a lot of money for CLIC Sargent who supported young children suffering the terrible effects of cancer. This was despite the seizures and being told by countless people that I must have been completely mad to have even attempted the event. Although I did hobble around for the following week on legs that felt as though they were made of glass!

One important lesson that I also learnt from this event was that it didn't matter if I came first over the finish line, or last. The main thing was that I took part and had the absolute satisfaction of knowing that I had completed it.

Over the previous four months of training I had learnt to turn negative thoughts and feelings into positive ones, which on its own helped me feel so much better and overcome so many obstacles, as well as becoming a more confident and fitter person than I had been before.

Another big issue I had to address through having the radiotherapy was that when I started to seize, I also lost both my sense of taste and smell.

Eventually everything that I ate became completely tasteless and at the worst of times all food left a metallic or peppery sensation in the mouth.

It isn't until you lose these two vital senses that you appreciate them and realise how vital a part of your everyday life they are.

At one point I could have eaten absolutely anything, without actually seeing what I had consumed, and wouldn't have had a clue as to what it was.

For about six weeks I felt as though I had been robbed of half my life; I could neither taste or smell and had continuous painful seizures each and every night to contend with. But the positive side was that the radiotherapy had successfully done its intended job and whenever I started to feel negative or even sorry for myself I would pull myself back into reality and remember that I had been so lucky compared to some of the children and their families that I had seen. I now had a choice and it was completely up to me to make the most of it!

Slowly but surely my senses began to return. At first I was convinced that it was my memory playing tricks on the body and giving me false indications. But sure enough I gradually regained the luxury of being able to taste food along with the ability to smell, and remember the first scent of honeysuckle growing in a hedge along one of the local footpaths I often used.

Ever since, I have never taken my senses for granted and fully appreciate the joy that they give me.

After the Norton half back in June, I had stupidly become more complacent with myself because I had achieved what seemed an impossible goal. I gradually stopped all my training and began to slip back into my old style of living, which involved going to work and happily chilling out with Scooby.

The thought of ever running another half marathon couldn't have been further from my mind, especially when I looked back and reflected on how hard the first one had been.

Gradually over the next few months of July and August I noticed that I began to feel really lethargic and tired again. At first I put it down to the physical demands of work but then gradually but surely the seizures began to return, mainly during the long nights, causing me to lose more and more sleep until it started affecting me during the daytime as well.

While operating machinery, especially for hours on end, I

noticed that I would have great difficulty in walking properly afterwards, and it would take as long as ten minutes of other graft or walking until my body resumed normal physical functions again.

Because I had found, purely by accident, that running had helped to suppress the seizures, I knew deep down that I had to start training again, but really disliked this thought of having to run miles just as a cure.

My first attempt to get back into training involved cycling, which I enjoyed at first but soon found really frustrating, probably after having had a motor bike for several years.

After persevering with cycling for many weeks, and finding that I could have run up the hills faster, and with no improvement with the seizures which were now becoming more prolonged and intense, I decided to try swimming. I found this really demanding and was sure that it would burn off all the waste products that were forming in the body, causing the restriction on muscle movements, but after several weeks this seemed to be having very little or no effect on the seizures.

By this time I was starting to get really worried with the thoughts of being trapped within my own body again and not being able to indulge in, and enjoy, everyday life.

My last resort would be to go back on really strong medication again, but with that would come the climate of not feeling completely in control of the situation along with feeling sorry for myself again.

After days of self-pity which I tried to hide from Steve and Phil, I reluctantly started running again after remembering the families that I had seen in hospital.

Initially it was really hard trying to push myself through a couple of weeks of what seemed endless hell. I just didn't want to start running again and fought so hard to overcome all the negative thoughts that tried to stop me.

After a week of persevering, mostly running during the evenings around Westfield and Radstock, I gradually started to feel better. The seizures became less frequent so I gained more sleep and became a lot more agile again, especially at work, where I found to my amazement I could jump straight up onto the back of the lorry that I was driving at the time, just like I could the previous year.

This proved a very important point to me that running was the only form of exercise that would help to control and prevent the seizures. But I still didn't enjoy the boredom of running the streets night after night on my own and struggled to leave the house each evening. I would make up any excuse that I could rather than venture outside to run after work.

What I didn't realise at the time was that I needed a special goal again to focus on and distract myself from all the negativity that was creeping up within me.

Then, while driving back home early one Saturday morning listening to Radio Bristol, I heard Ali Vowles recruiting for the last runner to join her team for the Bristol half marathon that September.

The team would be representing the Children's Hospice South West (CHSW) charity, helping raise vital funds for the 'Babes big appeal', a project to build Charlton Farm in Wraxall, on the outskirts of Bristol. This would be the second and much needed children's hospice supporting the local area.

I immediately parked the car in the next available lay-by and frantically searched for my mobile phone which always seemed to have the habit of hiding from me when most needed. I fumbled across the small keypad with nervous fingers, praying that I had remembered the radio station phone number correctly.

After what seemed like endless seconds with hands trembling in anticipation, I finally heard a lady's voice answer asking if she could help.

A million and one crazy thoughts were going through my mind: Had I got the right number? Was I too late? Had the last runner's place already been taken? After all it was a huge area that this station covered and I couldn't possibly be the only one applying for this single vacancy.

On hearing a voice saying hello for the second time I quickly replied in a nervous voice whether I was speaking to Radio Bristol. I felt immense relief when she replied to say that it was, and then asked the most important question which was whether the last runners vacancy was still available.

When I heard it was, I can remember punching my hand into the air with sheer delight, then feeling the pain as it struck the car roof. I had completely forgot in all the excitement that I was still sitting inside the car!

After confirming all my details, I continued my journey home feeling a brand new sense of enthusiasm, especially when Ali announced my name live on air to be the last person joining her team.

This one act brought a fresh perspective to all my training. It was a new goal which I grasped hold of with open hands and immense determination. Long gone were all the negative thoughts about how hard the last half marathon proved to be.

Excitedly, I couldn't wait to tell my cousins about my new ambition, but unexpectedly was greeted by a wall of silence. It felt as though time had been frozen as they both stopped immediately in their tracks and stared uncomfortably back at me. Then, as though they had rehearsed this speech beforehand, they explained to me how, at the finish line of the last one I had told them explicitly that I would never run a half marathon ever again.

Phil eventually released a cheeky and reassuring grin back at me, while Steve, still shaking his head in disbelief, occupied himself by putting the kettle on to make us all a relaxing pot of tea.

With this new boost of enthusiasm, the training along with all the miles seemed so much easier than before and I soon began to feel the hunger to cover more miles as the countdown of each week progressed.

***

On August 1st I drove to London and from the outskirts caught the underground tube into the centre where I found myself amongst thousands of other runners all making their way to the start of the 2004 London 10K. Never had I ever imagined lining up with so many others to run a race which proved to be so different from the Norton half marathon.

On the circuit I felt really comfortable and enjoyed seeing London's landmarks, which proved to be a great distraction. Collecting my very first race medal at the finish, I stood amongst so many other runners phoning family and friends and I decided to ring Steve who was relieved to hear I had completed the run without any problems. Steve was always a person who worried about what crazy tasks I would take on next.

The next race that I took part in was held on September 5th in Reading with a 10K circuit around the town centre following part of the old canal.

This run seemed much harder and in a strange way longer than the London 10K, mainly because there were fewer participants which allowed for large open gaps on the circuit.

With my training I had been averaging seven to eight mile distances and my furthest training run had been ten miles. Despite less mileage, Reading 10K was a hard run because I had run it far quicker than ever before. This proved a really valuable lesson that I would have to really pace myself in a week's time while running the Bristol half marathon and not get too carried away with all the faster runners.

Before the start of the Bristol half I met radio presenter Ali Vowles for the first time. All the team had a really warm and friendly welcome from her and the Children's Hospice South West representatives, which instantly made us all feel relaxed.

After the group photographs had been taken, I felt so proud to be part of a team taking part in such a large event and for such a special cause.

The start line was massive with different areas displaying various predicted finishing times. Thousands of runners were swarming to get to their locations as I mingled in amongst them, contented to be near the back of the queue.

Up ahead we could hear the air horn signalling the start of the race, and after several minutes of slowly ambling forward we had the sudden freedom of eventually crossing the start line.

After passing a large sign displaying that we had already covered three miles, I realised that I was running far too fast and began to slow down. This felt discouraging as a great number of runners began to overtake me while looking so fit and confident as they vanished into the huge carpet of runners in the distance.

Running up the long stretch of the Portway leading out from the city centre – passing underneath Brunel's famous suspension bridge – seemed never ending, especially as you could see all the fast runners coming back down on the opposite side of the dual carriageway.

Every now and then I would catch a glimpse of one of our CHSW team members wearing the distinct blue logo on the front of their white running vest.

The crowds were amazing with all their support and helped us immensely to cover each challenging mile. As we approached the town centre a marker board displaying mile ten was hung high above the crowds. I then noticed everyone was running far quieter and concentrating a lot harder to cover the last long three-mile section.

Eventually I could see the beautiful sight of the long-awaited finish line ahead. With my legs screaming in protest for me to stop I felt a huge sense of relief as I passed over the line, listening to all the beeps coming from the timing chips as they automatically registered everyone's performance.

With buckled and weary legs, I ambled through the finishers funnel to collect my third medal and t-shirt before half heartedly resting under the shade of a nearby tree in Queen's Square and devouring a bottle of refreshing cold water.

After a long rest and watching all the other runners amble by with family and friends, I tried to raise my feet but noticed that my legs had almost entirely locked solid with lactic acid. I had totally forgotten the golden rule to stretch out and warm down the body.

Trying my best not to catch the attention of others around me I clasped firmly onto the trunk of a huge tree and hauled myself onto unrecognisable legs to see if I could step away while keeping my balance.

I couldn't help but think what sarcastic comment Phil would come out with if he could see me now. Despite all the pain coming from my legs, I still could manage a smile the more I thought about Phil.

While looking around to see if anyone was watching I bravely attempted to walk forwards. Following a quick shuffle I managed to go about five metres to the safety of a metal barrier that I clung on to for dear life.

The next hour was spent manoeuvering from street lamp to street lamp until I reached the pick up point for the park and ride bus service to take me out of Bristol.

Later that evening as I retrieved my race results from the laptop, I realised that I had run the Bristol circuit in 2h-15m, which was over half an hour quicker than I had run Norton half marathon only three months earlier.

Despite the immense aching coming from my legs and the overwhelming tiredness – along with the occasional swear word whenever I tried to move quickly – I now felt a complete sense of satisfaction that all my hard training had paid off.

LAUGHTER AND SORROW

In 2005, compared to the year before, I now enjoyed all my running activities and could see my times and distances improving the harder I trained. Looking back, I think that achieving the first three-mile target was the hardest to overcome and even now find that, when I coach complete beginners' groups, they are nearly all experiencing the same situation.

All the extra training mostly kept the seizures at bay, which in itself made me feel much more content and comfortable within myself.

In March 2005, I ran the Bath half marathon and although I didn't break the two hour target I had in mind, each event was gradually getting quicker.

With all my events I managed to raise sponsorship for the Children's Hospice South West charity and felt so lucky to be given the chance to raise funds for them.

As with all my runs Steve would be the first to donate a contribution and help collect money from others keen to support me. I can recall one day mentioning to him that I might want to run a full marathon; his reply is unprintable! He made it clear to me in no uncertain terms that he didn't agree with it and that I would end up killing myself in the process, so I thought it was a wise decision at the time to leave well enough alone.

What I did next was to actually reduce my mileage and aim to run shorter distances faster. This proved really successful in a lot of the local 10K's and when I entered the London 10K for the second time.

All seemed to be going well until I noticed that very gradually the seizures were beginning to return, especially overnight when I would wake up in agony feeling as though I was being crushed alive in my own body.

After struggling to get out of bed and manoeuvring down the steep stairs in the cottage, I would walk around – sometimes out into the cold night air – until usually, after about ten minutes, the pain would gradually subside and give me back complete freedom of movement again. Sometimes, if lucky, I could have a night completely free from this while on others it could repeat itself two or three times in a row.

After desperately trying different types of cross training to accompany the running programme, it seemed to make very little difference, which proved frustrating and also very worrying. Having been able to control what was happening to me before, it now felt as though I was starting to lose the battle.

I found the only solution to remain ahead would be to increase my mileage, so I refocused my schedules for the year ahead and included the Bristol half marathon again, but this time with the ambition of achieving a finishing performance of under two hours.

At work Steve was my partner. He had been working for the company many years before me and passed on so much knowledge about civil engineering which made it far easier for me to learn the trade. There are so many stories to tell about working with him and what we did to make the days more enjoyable. Work is so much easier when you can share a smile!

I can recall one day while we were both working in a large car park in Clevedon. The job entailed exposing two high voltage electricity underground 11,000kv cables.

After successfully completing the task in the late afternoon, we were both walking back across the car park to our lorry when suddenly a car reversed back out from its parking space without any warning and straight into Steve, knocking him over.

It then promptly drove back into the space where it had come from and out climbed an elderly lady who quickly enquired whether Steve was okay. As he struggled to get back onto his feet he told her in a really ruffled voice that she should look where she was going (this is the polite version!).

The lady then got back into her car and asked again if Steve was alright. Wanting her to leave him well alone, he replied "yes" and hobbled away towards the lorry. But before he could get out of the way, she reversed her car out again and struck him for a second time.

We both looked at each other in complete disbelief as the elderly lady again emerged from the car and asked if he was alright. On seeing that he was still hobbling around she offered to give him a lift to the local doctor's surgery, to which he replied that he had seen enough of her driving and that under no circumstances was he ever going to risk his life by getting into the car with her!

Quickly seeking sanctuary by sheltering in between two other parked cars he then prompted her, with both hands, to be on her way.

Apart from a severely dented sense of pride – along with a sore knee – he was fine until he got into the lorry. Awaiting us eagerly in the cab was Scooby, my springer spaniel, who just loved attention and enjoyed winding Steve up whenever he had the opportunity.

As soon as I started to drive home, it all started. It was is as if I had two stroppy teenagers sat next to me. First of all, Scooby would be sat bolt upright on the double seat next to Steve and decide to lean over on him with all his weight; the more Steve would push him back the more Scooby would lean into him. This would go on for several minutes, Steve cursing Scooby and Scooby growling back at Steve.

I would then curse the pair of them, which would lead to complete silence, but only for a few moments. Out of the corner of my eye I would watch as Scooby gradually raised his paw and slapped it firmly on the top of Steve's head, directly in the middle of his ever expanding bald patch! Steve would immediately then remove the offending paw before Scooby would repeat his action.

For anyone watching it must have looked as though the pair of them were having a boxing match.

Without warning, Steve suddenly rose out of his seat, and released a horrendous yell, banging his head on the cab roof. On enquiring what the hell he was playing at he explained that Scooby had put his paw firmly down on his bad knee, which I must admit did look really swollen.

The worst thing was that Scooby now knew this and every now and then on the long journey home would just check on Steve to see just how bad his knee was.

Finally, when we got back to the work's yard and were about to go home, Steve couldn't find his mobile phone anywhere. We both searched the lorry cab high and low but to no avail. When I later got home and went through the daily routine of washing out my vacuum flask and lunch box, I then found Steve's mobile phone complete with Scooby's teeth marks in the depths of my works bag!

On another occasion while we were looking for some building supplies in the tool section of a warehouse in Taunton I found a really long sink plunger.

Having only seen these before in comic books that I used to read as a kid, curiosity got the better of me and I started to wonder how strong the dome shaped rubber end actually stuck to shiny surfaces.

There was only one way to find out, so as I followed Steve up through the narrow aisles, I promptly picked up the plunger and pushed it down on his shiny bald patch.

It was a hot day and I couldn't believe how effective this plunger could be. With a lot of swearing I could see him frantically trying to remove it.

First of all he tried to remove it by pulling on the long wooden handle with one hand, only to find it wasn't going to budge an inch. Then he tried both hands which resulted in his head turning into an acorn shape, completely distorting his facial features like something out of a horror film.

I really didn't think that it was going to come off and under all the snarling I heard him mutter something about if it didn't, that I would be the one paying for it. I tried my hardest not to smile as I pictured him queuing up at the checkout, or even worse walking across the car park like a telly tubby.

Finally with the help of a sales assistant, who was in tears of laughter, they managed to rotate the rubber base and pull it down over his eyes where it released itself with a loud pop, only to leave a rather large red patch on the top of his head, resembling the look of a huge love bite!

***

It was an ordinary Monday morning in June when Steve joined me early in the work yard to set about our daily duties. As usual I commented that the weekends were never long enough and had again passed by so quickly. He replied by saying that time couldn't have passed by quick enough for him, as he had been in so much pain from his shoulder.

On asking what he had done to it, he said that he had woken up with a severe pain in his left shoulder ever since Saturday morning. Although the pain had subsided a little, he was now still in a lot of discomfort.

We carried on loading our truck, but I could see from the expression on his face that he was still in a great deal of pain even though he tried to hide it from me. So I suggested that he should go and get it checked out with his doctor. Immediately he protested that he didn't have the time to spare to mess around seeing any doctor, so I let him carry on and help finish the loading.

When he then lifted his lunch bag into the cab of the truck to leave, I could immediately see from his reactions that he was clearly suffering. I knew that he ate a lot of food, but it couldn't have been that heavy!

So I switched off the engine and told him that he wasn't going any further unless he promised to phone his GP for an appointment. After a lot of mumbling under his breath he finally agreed that at 8am when the surgery opened he would phone them.

On arriving in Clevedon an hour later and keeping a close eye on the time I had to pester him even more until he reluctantly made the call.

After he refused for me to drive him anywhere, he confirmed that his appointment would be at 10am that morning, so I off-loaded the tools required for the next few hours and told him to leave to make sure he arrived at the doctor's surgery on time.

Another worker, Len, drove down on site to help cover while Steve was away. We both agreed that he must have been in a lot of pain to go and see any doctor. He was simply one of those fellows who would go for years on end without visiting their GP or even remember what they looked like.

Several hours went by while it was in the back of my mind, constantly niggling away that they might find something majorly wrong with him.

Finally, at 2pm Steve returned to site looking really worried. The immediate impression that I had was that something seriously wrong had been found with him, but it turned out that he was more worried about not being back on site, rather than his own health.

Both Len and I quickly questioned him in the hope that he was okay to which he replied that he was really annoyed that the doctors had mixed up his father's medical prescription and lost him a lot of time, otherwise he would have returned a lot sooner than he had. Prompting him again he casually said that the doctor had told him he had torn a muscle in his shoulder and to keep an eye on his blood pressure as it was higher than normal. I felt so relieved to hear this and slowly began to relax once more.

For the rest of the afternoon I see could that his shoulder was giving him a lot of pain, purely from the expression on his face. Steve would never complain about how bad he felt. He would just soldier on and discreetly take a few more painkillers to try and settle himself.

On leaving the yard that evening, I told him to take it steady and look after himself. I knew full well that wasn't going to happen because he was looking after his elderly father and would probably be doing all the washing and cooking once he got back home.

The next morning, I picked Steve up from his home to save him driving up to the yard and back, which would hopefully give him some valuable spare time at home to catch up on all the daily chores. As he climbed into the truck, I could see that he was still in a lot of pain and asked him how his evening had gone. He quietly explained that he had been up for most of the night tending to his father, so he had very little sleep and was feeling really tired.

Throughout the day he took more than the usual number of breaks to seek rest, which was totally out of character for him. I suggested that he should at least go back and see his doctor again, to which he gave no reply.

Not wanting to pester him any more after seeing that he really was exhausted, I didn't mention it to him again, after all it probably was the sleepless nights and visit to the doctor that added to his current condition. I certainly didn't want to annoy him any further than I already had. When I dropped Steve off at home that evening, I told him that if he needed any help with anything he should phone me any time of the night.

Early the next morning I had a phone call from him saying that he felt so tired that he wasn't coming in to work and that he would phone me later in the day to let me know how he was feeling.

I thought to myself that I had hardly ever known him to take a day off sick from work and began to worry even more. But then I knew Steve and if I kept on at him by asking questions it would upset him and make him feel even worse than he did. So I gave him the chance to have a good rest and hopefully catch up on some sleep before I phone him again later.

After arriving back home that evening and quickly getting most of my daily chores out of the way, I thought that I'd give Steve a ring to see how he was. I didn't phone him during the day as I wasn't sure if he would be catching up on sleep and didn't want to disturb him, after all he promised that if he needed anything he would phone me.

Pouring myself a cup of tea, the phone then rang and I thought he had beaten me to it, but instead of Steve it was Phil, in a total state of panic. He explained that something was wrong with Steve and that he would be coming round to pick me up so we could go and see him in person.

Minutes later we were on our way, and on arrival came the biggest shock to both of us.

We quickly learnt that Steve had cooked an evening meal for his father and sat down to have a quick nap while relaxing in the chair. Later on when his father tried to wake him, he found that Steve had peacefully died in his sleep.

The shock was indescribable, it was the last thing that I had ever expected to hear, especially at such a young age.

The outcome was that Steve had died from acute heart disease, which apparently had been affecting him for some time. This was a huge loss, which felt as though it had left a gaping hole in all our lives. One of the closest people to me had suddenly gone forever.

A LONG WAY UP

Later in the year, I ran both the London and Reading 10K's again, but this time I just didn't seem to have the same enthusiasm as before. I really missed Steve telling me to be careful before my races and the several phone calls that I would get afterwards to hear my results, so I never ran them again.

I still continued to train hard on my own, during the evenings after work, and enjoyed my running sessions which helped relieve a lot of the pain and frustration from losing Steve.

On many occasions I would forget and lift the phone just to give him a quick call, then suddenly the cruel reality would grasp hold of me and bring me sharply back into the real world.

A memory that kept niggling away at me was that whenever I previously mentioned to him that I was thinking of running a full marathon, he would quickly dismiss the idea as entirely impossible.

With this in mind I went to visit Phil and discuss the idea to see what he thought about it. I can remember the look on his face when I suggested it and mentioned that I would also like to run it on Stephen's birthday in October. With a cheeky grin on his face, he looked directly at me and said "that's twice as far as you've ever run before, and we all know how long that took you".

That was it, he knew that if I had someone who doubted what I could do, I would do everything that I could to prove them wrong.

Days later, after scrolling through all the running magazines that I could find and searching the internet for a marathon that I could run on Saturday 29th October 2005, there appeared to be only one result: Snowdonia.

Phil just kept laughing and laughing when I finally told him. Then the laughing gradually subsided when he saw that I was serious about taking on this event.

Looking at me directly in the face, as if wishing I would suddenly start laughing and say "only joking", he slowly and quietly said "You are serious, aren't you?". To which I replied "Deadly serious", as I watched his face reluctantly relax, gently rubbing his chin with one hand in total silence while propping himself up against the fireplace.

"Don't doubt you can do it", came back a quick reply, "you always were a determined little sod."

October 29th would have been Steve's 46th birthday and instead of hanging around and missing him, I felt as though I wanted to do something constructive to remember him by and help distract and refocus others that knew him as well.

With the Snowdonia marathon booked it was now time to get the training on schedule, with only three months to go until the day of the race.

My seizures had started to increase again, with some nights being better than others. Night times were always the worst for me when the body was in a state of rest. The seizures would settle into all my muscles, causing them to tighten up and eventually wake me from the depths of sleep into a sudden world of pain. This could happen as many as three times during one night.

Many a time I would curse and think to myself, "why me?", before remembering the children and their families while I was in hospital. It would remind me how lucky I was, as I still had the choice of being able to walk the seizures free from my body after 10 to 15 minutes of continuous movement.

With more training, especially over the weekends, the seizures gradually began to subside again. It was a great relief being able to have a decent night's sleep. Instead of training only on the local roads, I would run the hilly 10-mile section into Bath city centre and the huge climb up over Widcombe Hill and then return on the same route home again. Knowing just how hilly the Snowdonia circuit was, it was my plan to incorporate as many hills as possible into my training programs.

I had just returned home from training one evening when I heard someone frantically knocking on my front door. On opening I found it was Phil looking really worried, as if he had all the troubles of the world stacked on his shoulders.

Later while sitting down with a mug of tea firmly clenched in his hand, along with an intense stare, he proceeded to tell me that he had been in hospital earlier where he had been diagnosed with having cancer of the liver. His focus never left me, as if looking for a positive reaction during the explanation. If only I could reassure him that all would be okay. Perhaps by some miracle they had got the diagnosis wrong.

I couldn't believe what he was telling me, but knew deep down that I couldn't let him see my true reaction because he always looked to me as being strong.

After many questions and trying to reassure Phil on many issues, he seemed a lot more relaxed in himself and several hours later left far more positive than when he had arrived. Later that evening as darkness fell, the reality of what was going on to those closest to me began to take hold, leaving me with very little sleep.

A week later Phil had a major operation to remove the cancerous growth from his liver and awaited further treatment along with the the outcome of his results. It felt so good to get him back home from the hospital and feel as though we were all back together again.

In what seemed like no time at all, October arrived and I began to taper down the training during the last few weeks leading up to the marathon. I felt really good, strong and confident in my mind, taking on such a new and demanding challenge.

I packed my tent and all the gear needed into the car on the Thursday evening and arranged for Phil to look after my dogs, Scooby and Bonnie, while I was away.

After finishing work on the Friday evening, I started the long drive up to Snowdonia. It was dark and the skies emptied torrential rain throughout the whole journey.

During the final section of the long winding roads down into Llanberris, I was greeted by masses of leaves falling onto the windscreen, assisted by gale force winds and persistent rain that sent torrents of flood water down either side of the steep road. Every now and then I could hear the floodwater as it changed direction from one side of the road to the other.

Eventually I arrived at the outskirts of Llanberris, where my initial plan was to set up camp for the night. I just about managed to force the driver's car door open against the immensely strong winds that now gusted ferociously up through the valley separating the mountains. Giving in to the wind I let the car door close on me and lowered the driver's seat right back, so that I could stretch out my legs from the journey while staying dry.

The wind grew even stronger, rocking the car from side to side, making the thought of even erecting a tent in these conditions seem impossible. So I drove on down into the main village where all the shops were and settled for a huge portion of fish and chips, before driving to a remote car park next to the lake. Here I parked between two other cars to try and seek some shelter then settled down for the evening, folding down all the seats. I was then gently rocked to sleep by the force of the elements outside, helped immensely by the tiredness of the long journey after finishing work.

As the sun began to rise in the early morning sky, golden rays of light delicately lit up the sides of the valleys all around. The dark and ferocious sky from the previous evening had now passed, leaving behind a tranquil blue sky that stretched as far as the eye could see.

Winding the car seats back into position, I could now sit and appreciate this magnificent view that greeted me.

After several minutes I decided that it would look far better if I had a fresh brew of tea in my hand, so I opened the door, remembering how difficult it had been the night before, and clambered out into the car park.

It took a while to straighten up the old body properly, and I felt more than happy to wander and stand for a while, before the whistle of the kettle told me that my stove had boiled the water.

Several brews later, along with a carton of porridge, I began to feel so grateful that the dreadful weather had now passed. All that remained from it now was a large deposit of gravel on the outer edge of the car park, along with an endless supply of autumn-coloured leaves that delicately floated on the surface of several huge puddles nearby.

In no time at all, there seemed to be an endless stream of cars now entering Llanberris, quickly replacing the peace and tranquillity, with the sound of people getting ready for the marathon.

As the numbers rapidly grew, I got changed into my running gear, collected my race number and joined the crowds of runners, most of them in nervous conversation as they made their way to the start line.

Pre-race nerves now greeted me as I looked up the steep road that led out of Llanberris. I couldn't really appreciate how steep it was the evening before because of the reduced vision from the torrential rain.

The climb out of the village seemed to take forever. The unforgiving steep gradient lasted for an eternal four miles. I can remember commenting to a fellow runner, who ran at the same pace as myself, "will this hill ever come to an end?".

Eventually we ran over the ridge of the long road and were greeted by a magnificent view overlooking the Snowdonia countryside in all her beauty. The bright sunlight now exposed every colour imaginable as it cast its rays over the lush green valleys below. On our right-hand side as we descended, we could clearly see the summit of Snowdonia reaching far into the sky.

It seemed an extremely long race at the time. As we passed crowds in remote villages our spirits would suddenly be raised by their generous support. But out on the more remote sections of the run I found it hard to focus on my pace. Increasing tiredness and severe fatigue began to take over my body. My mind would lose all concentration and one minute I would be looking at the amazing and beauty of the countryside, the next I would be thinking of Steve.

What comments would he be coming out with now? Perhaps he was right? I was only at mile 21. Had I taken on far too much? Would I collapse in an embarrassing heap in the middle of the road?

With all this commotion going on in my head, I hadn't realised just how much my pace had dramatically dropped, I was now running as fast as a very slow walk.

From behind me I could hear loud footsteps approaching at a dramatic rate. I didn't want to look behind so instead tried to refocus on my speed to keep them at bay. Slowly but surely the offending competitor caught me and slowly began to overtake. To my astonishment it turned out to be an American postman wearing bright red uniform and boots, complete with a large leather satchel and huge smile, as he sailed by into the distance.

Instead of tormenting myself with the remaining distance to run, I began to reward myself with every mile that I had gained. Slowly I began to feel a lot more comfortable, and less runners passed me as I kept up with several small groups.

I lost count of how many times I must have cursed Steve during the run and questioned why it had to be Snowdonia for my first marathon. But at the same time, rewarded myself for taking on such a massive challenge.

I could now see and hear in the far distance the finish line. The commentator's megaphone was really clear to us at times, but became a lot less distinctive at others, especially when we descended down through little country lanes enclosed by tall trees still holding onto their autumn coloured leaves.

Just as we thought we were approaching the finish line, the marshals then guided us away in the opposite direction. We had to run up over another really steep hill, which so cruelly tormented everyone both physically and psychologically. This was when a large number of runners, who suddenly saw the hill before them, simply stopped in their tracks in disbelief.

My legs refused even to attempt to run this last hill. I had to resort to very small steps up the incline, pushing off my knees with each hand on every step taken.

At times I stopped to regain my breath, in a desperate attempt to feed my lungs with cool fresh air, then amble on again upwards in the hope that I would soon reach the top. With my legs now screaming at me to stop, I began the painful descent, that proved just as hard as the incline.

Carefully avoiding all the rocks protruding from the long grass, each and every muscle in my legs felt as though they were being ripped apart from the continuous impact of running downhill on the uneven ground.

The finish line was now definitely within sight as I finished the last elusive mile that so reluctantly surrendered its torment. I crossed the finish line to a fantastic response from all the spectators in a time of 4 hours-45 minutes.

I felt so glad to finish, after what seemed an eternity of running, I could now actually relax and reflect on all the lonely hours of training that had gone into this.

Picking up my engraved slate plaque to commemorate the marathon, I treasured it within the firm grasp of my hands as if it were the crown jewels themselves.

I slowly shuffled amongst all the other competitors to retrieve my kit bag and quietly but clumsily got dressed, so as not to get cold. It felt so good to change out of my soaking wet running gear into the comfort of ordinary clothes.

After attempting a few very poor and measly stretching exercises, I made my way into a huge marquee where cakes and refreshments were on hand to all those competing that day. Sitting within arm's reach of both the large tea urn and a huge selection of home baked cakes, I felt as though I had landed in Heaven. A kind fellow who must have noticed how badly I was walking gave up his seat for me and transferred to one further back.

It was now starting to get really cold and the hot cup of tea in my hands both tasted and felt good from the warmth that it generated. The lady who was endlessly serving out all the mugs of tea, smiled radiantly at me as I cautiously asked for my third refill, which equalled the number of slices of delicious cake that I had so gratefully demolished.

Deep in thoughts looking back over the run, I was suddenly distracted by the ringing of my mobile phone. It was Phil checking that I was okay and seeing if I had survived the run. On answering I noticed that he had made three previous calls, all before I had finished the race.

"Where the heck have you been?" was his initial reaction. Then when I quickly explained that I had only just got back in from the finish, he further enquired if I had got lost on the way round, before breaking out into a familiar chuckle. It felt great to hear his voice; tears started to well up in my eyes as he told me how proud Steve would have been of me. "So, what time will you be home?" he enquired eagerly. I promised him that I would phone when I was ready to leave and let him know.

After several conversations with other runners about how their run had gone that day, I decided that it was time to leave so that I could drive back before darkness fell and be home for a reasonable time. As I tried to raise myself from the comfort of the chair, it suddenly became apparent that my legs were refusing to co-operate with the rest of my body, so I quickly sat back down to avoid any embarrassment from those around me.

Taking a deep breath and quickly standing on my feet, my arms shot violently out as I tried to support myself, balancing both arms on the chair. Standing bolt upright and pretending that everything was okay, I quickly ordered another mug of tea. "Are you alright?" enquired the tea lady, looking at me with her head slightly tilted to one side.

"Yeah, fine thanks," I replied, "just a bit of stiffness in the ol' legs from the run, but I'll soon walk that off in a minute."

As I drank my fourth mug of tea, propped up against the serving counter, I gently started to move one leg at a time, while at the same time eyeing up my escape route from the marquee, feeling like an escaped convict, hoping not to be caught.

Now with my mug devoid of every drop of tea there was no choice but to make a break for it. On watching a few other runners cross before me – also struggling to walk properly – I quickly decided to join them in the hope that I would blend in and not look half as bad as I felt. As I grabbed my bag to make an exit, one of the handles had managed to tangle itself under the chair leg, tipping it over as I struggled forwards, bringing immediate attention to myself. Placing the chair back upright, I shuffled out of the marquee in the hope of keeping up with the others who had now disappeared from sight.

Once outside I felt the freedom from all the embarrassment and gave myself short targets to walk to until I reached the car park. It was then that I realised that that there was no way that I could drive home in such a condition and proceeded to place my bag into the back of the car.

A couple next to me who were just getting into their car asked if I was staying the night. I told them I was just relaxing my legs a little before attempting to drive back home.

"What we do to relieve the pain and stiffness from the legs is to walk to the top of Snowdonia the following morning". With a huge smile on both their faces I could see that they were awaiting my response.

"You've got to be joking" was my immediate reply. I couldn't think of anything worse or more painful to do.

Their expressions quickly changed from a smile to one of complete seriousness as they explained: "No, it works everytime. Meet us at the bottom by the little railway station at 9am if you wish to join us".

As I painfully lowered myself into the car, I pondered as to whether they were actually being serious or just cruelly making fun of me.

Having made the decision not to drive home that evening, I phoned Phil to explain the situation, but avoided telling him I had slept in the car the previous night, and would be doing the same for a second evening – I was in no fit state to start erecting a tent!

Before I got too settled I managed to stagger into the village and saw that the local café would be open at 8am, so I would be okay for a good breakfast. I then proceeded back to the car with a large take-away meal to celebrate completing the run.

My final view of the day was watching the sun slowly set down behind the distant mountain range, taking with her the last golden rays of light as they disappeared from the reflection on the lake, that stretched out before me.

It was a peaceful but very restless night sleeping in the car. One minute my feet would be up on the dashboard the next they would be over on the passenger seat while trying to avoid the gear stick. But eventually I managed to settle down in a sleeping bag along with an oversized belly resulting from the large take-away meal.

With fresh sunlight now pouring in through the car windows, which were heavily coated in condensation, I gradually woke up and regained my senses.

After several minutes of laying still and reflecting on the day before, I decided that I needed to stretch out and get the faithful kettle back on for a fresh brew of tea.

Managing to half free one hand from the sleeping bag, which now felt more like a strait jacket, I managed to open the car door. I immediately regretted this as I slid unceremoniously out of the car and landed heavily onto the floor.

Struggling to free myself from the sleeping bag, I managed with one hand to grasp hold of the open door and tug myself up onto my feet. My first reaction was to look around me to see if anyone had seen. Luckily, no one had, and I proceeded to quickly wipe away the dirt and gravel from my head!

With the welcome sound of the kettle singing away as it puffed clouds of steam into the fresh morning air, I soon had a brew going, which helped me to forget my earlier escapade.

Leaving the car I made my way very slowly towards the village to find its amazing café where I ordered the largest breakfast that I could, to set me up for the long day ahead.

Gazing from the café window it was easy to spot the people who had run the marathon as they made their way painfully up through the high street.

As I emptied the last pot of tea, I reflected on what the couple had told me the evening before about joining them for a walk up Snowdonia to relieve the legs. If I was to leave the comfort of the café now, I should just about make it to the railway kiosk in time to join them or I could simply stay here, order another pot of tea and relax for an hour but suffer from really sore legs.

I decided that it was more important to get the legs sorted, otherwise the long journey home would be nothing short of hell.

As I waited by the kiosk, I did wonder if they had me on some wild goose chase, until they appeared from around the corner, both hobbling in the same state as myself. And after a lot of reassurance, we were all on our way to the summit of Snowdonia. Several times Phil rang on my mobile to see how things were progressing. When I explained to him what I was doing he thought I was joking, until I lost the telephone signal!

My legs at first just protested and I really didn't think I would be able to carry on up the steep ascent. I felt so tired and in so much pain that I almost dismissed the whole thing as rediciculous. But as I continued each painful step, they gradually eased until I could form a reasonable pace and no longer needed to push myself off my knees by using my arms for momentum.

On reaching the summit, I thanked the other two who, in return, thanked me for joining them. The whole area was surrounded by thick fog which denied us all the magnificent views that we would have seen, had we been up there the day before.

On the way down, we regained the views of the surrounding countryside which lay out before us, and also the telephone signal. Phil was now eagerly asking how quick I would be before I got home.

My legs had certainly benefitted from the climb and I had regained the freedom back into them, which made me feel a lot more comfortable for driving back home.

About halfway back, I drove into a service station to refuel and promptly opened the door to attend the fuel pump. As I tried to get out of the car, I suddenly realised that my legs refused to do anything. Hauling myself out by hanging off the petrol pump I proceeded to fill up. When I then attempted to pay at the kiosk it didn't matter how hard I tried to hobble in a straight line towards it, I would suddenly veer off in one direction then another. The more I tried to correct myself the worse it became.

When I eventually paid for the fuel and an armful of goodies for the journey home, I thought that I had better explain my behaviour to the cashier who had seen my erratic walking, just in case she thought I had been drinking and reported me.

Driving the car away from the pumps and parking up, I gave myself a good walk for 20 minutes until I felt much better again then continued my journey home.

I couldn't have been home for any more than a couple of minutes when there was an impatient knocking on the door. It was Phil and his wife Val who had arrived complete with a bottle of champagne and a whole array of foods to celebrate our achievement. This was why I had so many phone calls. Not only were they worried about me getting back safely but they wanted to make sure that we all celebrated and raised our glasses for a very special toast to Steve.

MISSING A PART OF YOURSELF

In 2006 Phil regularly had treatment to try and halt the spread of cancer that had now moved from his liver to infect other regions of his body. The main thing that continued to inspire me was his constant positive attitude and great spirit that he shared with all those around him.

I continued with regular training intervals on my own, trying to train harder and faster, which at times proved really difficult after finishing long hours at work. What really didn't help was when I found myself sat comfortably in a large armchair, mug of tea in hand, with the temptation to just fall into a deep sleep.

But the reality remained that if I didn't train hard then the dreaded seizures would return and I wouldn't be fit enough to do anything.

I gave myself several goals throughout this year by entering more running events like the Swindon half marathon, in the hope that I would break my two-hour completion time. As hard as I tried, I couldn't quite achieve this and felt really disillusioned when I missed my target by just 10 seconds. For hours after the run I questioned what I could have done to have erased those vital 10 seconds; perhaps if I had run past a water station instead of slowing down for it, or could I have just pushed that little bit harder?

When I later ran the Bristol half marathon in September, I was quite adamant that I was going to beat my old time and achieve my goal of completing the run in under two hours.

All through the event, I ran as fast as I possibly could, looking ahead for gaps in the runners so that I wouldn't be held up or boxed-in during the race.

When the finish line finally appeared in the distance and I could hear the welcome sound of the commentator, I couldn't believe my time; it was 11 minutes slower than I had ran earlier in Swindon. I felt so frustrated with myself again, and just couldn't understand why I was getting slower and not increasing my speed, especially with all the effort that I had put in. What I didn't realise at the time, or had completely overlooked, was the fact that I had been so lucky to be able to run at all. I should've rewarded myself for completing such a challenge and being able to raise a lot of money for the Children's Hospice South West appeal, to help build Charlton Farm.

Continually while out training Phil would phone me enquiring as to where I was and often unexpectedly appear with refreshments to support me. Very often he would pass the comment, "call yourself a runner?" as I stood before him, sweat dripping down my face.

In March 2007 the Bath half marathon was upon me. I had trained reasonably well, but not as much as I wish I had done come race day. Again, I failed to beat the two-hour barrier, but wasn't completely surprised seeing that I had been pretty casual with my training regime.

This also reflected on the amount of seizures I now had to endure. I soon realised that I needed to increase my training again if I were to keep them under control.

Phil now seemed to be less positive and totally fed up with his continuous treatment. I could tell by the way that he lost his sense of enthusiasm, and the sparkle in his smile slowly started to disappear.

We would regularly go out for a beer and chat endlessly about everything and anything. He was one of those people who – it didn't matter where we went – he would always end up meeting someone he knew.

One evening I had a phone call from Phil sounding really disillusioned with himself. He asked if I would be at home later that evening so he could come round and have a talk about something that was worrying him.

He explained to me while on the phone, that while at work for the last couple of days, he had been finding it hard to walk and was so short of breath, that he was now struggling to complete his daily tasks.

When he then came to the front door he looked extremely concerned and full of life's worries. I quickly explained to him that I had to walk my dogs, Bonnie and Scooby, as I had just got home. So I gave him Scooby to walk while I held onto little Bonnie. Scooby was always the most active of the two dogs and I knew he would help to pull Phil along!

While walking and chatting, Phil offloaded his problems, and explained to me how hard he found it to walk and the difficulty he now had with his breathing. I reached out and caught hold of Scooby's lead bringing them both to a sudden halt, and calmly looking at Phil directly in the face, told him that he had just walked a mile and a half without stopping or being short of breath. "You know, you're right" he replied, with the distinctive grin only Phil could give.

"But how did you cope when you were going through your treatment?" he eagerly asked. I explained to him how the running helped to make me feel so much better and control the seizures during the night, when the body felt most relaxed.

We then both agreed that if Phil was to start running, I would support and guide him to see if it helped him to feel any better.

For several weeks we trained together, starting with very short runs and progressing gradually onto longer targets. Because I had reduced my mileage, the seizures gradually but surely returned, so I had to give Phil a training programme that he could do on his own, while I continued with my longer runs. Occasionally we would run together, which I thoroughly enjoyed, especially with the banter that we would give each other.

He then set himself the target to run the Norton half marathon, exactly the same as I had done some three years earlier, which suddenly gave him a goal to aim for.

But about a month later, I had a call from him saying that he was really struggling to train and just couldn't find the drive or ambition to carry on with it. Because he had it set in his mind that he just wasn't improving enough, he didn't want to give up, but at the same time felt that he didn't want to run anymore.

I explained to him that this was a common experience, especially when people start to feel anxious about what they have taken on and worry themselves silly over it.

It was then that I threw him the gauntlet that I knew he wouldn't refuse. I explained to him that what he was trying to achieve now, against what I had managed to cover so far, was the equivalent of him trying to run 100 miles.

So, I promised him there and then – out a state of sheer madness – that if he completed the Norton half marathon, I would run 100 miles! His face was a picture of sheer delight as he immediately shook the living daylight out of my hand as his distinctive grin reappeared. "This calls for a whiskey" he replied and with a totally new attitude, toasted our challenge while staring at each other in a state of disbelief. Tilting his head to one side and giving a huge wink he swiftly emptied the remainder of his glass.

The following day as I woke up, the first thought that sprung to mind was my conversation with Phil, which brought a strange feeling of both nervousness and excitement.

Throughout the following months, Phil had a far greater sense of determination in his voice and I could see when we met each other that his whole face was now full of excitement, even though he was still receiving very strong treatment to control the spread of cancer.

During those months I also had to increase my training to prepare for a marathon in May at Lake Windemere, which was fast approaching.

On Friday 18th May, I packed the car and drove up to the Lake District with all my camping gear. When I arrived it was a beautiful day and I couldn't believe how stunningly beautiful the countryside was. I just felt so lost in this incredible landscape and knew that I would have to start exploring it immediately.

Booking into a campsite on the shores of Lake Windemere, I quickly set up the tent, which would be my home for the next couple of days, and settled down for the evening. The lake sat so still like a millpond that evening, with only the calling of distant ducks every now and then breaking the silence. Sitting outside the tent, I watched as the sun gently disappeared along with all the stunning colour on the surrounding hills.

After a comfortable night's sleep, I awoke to another gorgeous day of beautiful warm sunshine, which quickly drove the remaining mist from the surface of the lake.

After deciding to have a large breakfast to fuel myself up for the morning and increase my strength for the marathon ahead, I buttered up six large baps and placed them on a little picnic table in the entrance of the tent. I then proceeded to cook a whole pack of sausages along with a pack of bacon in the extra-large frying pan. The crackle and smell from the early morning fry up made me feel even hungrier than when I started. In order not to smell the tent out, I cooked all this outside in the fresh air, where I could enjoy the magnificent views that stretched for miles on end, across all the peaks and surrounding mountains.

When everything in the pan had cooked, I quickly added a full kettle to the stove and walked back across the few metres of grass which led to the entrance of the tent. On arrival I saw a duck, promptly leaving with one of my baps firmly gripped in its beak. With its head held high and little legs running as fast as they could, it took off to the nearby shore and swam out across the lake to be greeted by several other of its mates, who were also enjoying a selection of buttered baps!

I chased after it, complete with a frying pan full of sausages and bacon, but had no chance of catching the little devil.

Returning to the tent, there stood an empty plate on the table top, to which I could only smile and think to myself that it could have been worse, they could have pinched the sausages!

I spent the rest of the day driving around admiring the beautiful countryside. On spotting a magnificent waterfall, pouring out from the side of one of the hills, I found a lay-by in which to park and climbed up across the rugged hillside to investigate. Sudden gusts of wind would sweep up through the valley, which would at times lift sections of the water, making it look as if it was travelling back upwards into the sky from where it had previously fallen.

As the evening fell, I felt really tired from all the steep walks, but really comfortable as I remembered all the incredible sights from the day's outing.

The following morning as I cooked breakfast, I made sure that all my bread rolls remained in the safety of the closed tent. I couldn't help but feel as though I was being watched, and on turning around to investigate, saw six ducks in a line all innocently watching every movement that I made. Relaxing back into the comfort of a cosy fold-up chair and tucking into another huge freshly cooked breakfast, the ducks silently milled around my feet waiting for the slightest crumb to fall to the ground. Just for their sheer cheekiness, I gave them a large bread roll, which in pieces, they sped off with to the water's edge and out onto the vast lake.

Just before I was about to collect my race number, my phone rang; it was Phil. He wanted to wish me good luck on the run and asked me to let him know how I got on afterwards. I couldn't help but notice that there was a distinct change in his voice, instead of being the really happy fellow that he always portrayed, the tone was that of sadness. Perhaps he just wasn't feeling well at that particular moment and would be better later on.

With the sun shining down from a clear blue sky, I was really enjoying the marathon. The circuit went around the whole perimeter of Lake Windemere, taking us through several stunning little villages, which had quaint stone bridges spanning both small and large crystal-clear rivers.

During the run I was constantly distracted by the colourful tourist boats that gently cruised across the huge lake, forming small tidal waves that rippled over the deep blue surface.

Small crowds would cheer us on in random places, which would bring me back into reality and help me focus again on the race. At the top of a small hill, in a secluded lay-by, an ice cream van handed out fresh cones of fluffy cold ice cream, that looked so tempting to stop for.

Four hours and 45 minutes later, I crossed over the finish line and immediately made my way over to the refreshments marquee to cool down and seek shelter from the hot sun. This time I felt so much better than in Snowdonia. My legs did ache but nowhere near as bad as they had done previously, and I could talk to fellow runners while still standing and feel reasonably comfortable.

I phoned Phil to let him know that I had finished and would soon be on my way home. Again I could tell from his voice that something wasn't right, which started to concern me. I knew deep down I should get back to see him.

I quickly packed up the tent, which I had left erected in case I couldn't drive back again on the same day, and was relieved to see that I hadn't been raided while away by my local feathered friends.

Phil's condition over the next few weeks rapidly deteriorated. All I could do was try to reassure him about everything. Never had I ever felt so helpless. Normally I could resolve most things, but this I couldn't, which I found so frustrating.

On June 6th, I received a call from Val to tell me Phil had been rushed to hospital. On arriving I joined him and his family who were gathered around.

Firmly clutching his hand, I told him quietly how proud I was of him before he gently passed away.

That evening I sat on the edge of my bed, head lowered in both hands, in floods of tears, and began to reflect on so many thoughts and memories, until darkness fell around me.

I kept questioning relentlessly why the two closest people to me had been so cruelly taken away. Two really good, honest men who enjoyed life and wouldn't think twice about helping anyone.

Memories came flooding back, like the time when young Scooby, excited to see Phil one day, jumped up into the chair with him and promptly peed into his lap. On hearing all the commotion going on, I ran in from the kitchen to find Phil stood in the middle of my living room in just his under pants clutching a soggy pair of jeans, in full view of the window for anyone to see while passing by.

Over the following week I changed, my personality became bitter and I developed a much harsher outlook on life. I would often think of my very first race when Phil and Steve had so patiently waited for me. Out of the three of us, I was the one who was unwell at that time, not them, so why was I the one who was still here?

On the day of the funeral, I decided to give a short talk about some of the memories that I wanted to share. Never before would I have ever contemplated giving a talk to others, especially in a church full of people. But I wanted to keep hold of Phil in some way and not let him go.

I can remember shaking like a leaf, with my notes clutched in my sweaty hands. But my determination remained and somehow I managed to say what I wanted, in order to represent him as best as I could.

Phil had died just two weeks before the Norton half marathon and the decision was made to run with both my running number and Phil's along with a photo of him, supporting that contagious smile of his around the circuit. A very close friend of his for many years, Jane, agreed to run with me and represent him by carrying his photo.

During the race, which I thought would be relatively easy compared to the marathons I had ran, I found it hard to keep up with Jane as she ran all the hills with ease. On several occasions she would patiently wait for me to catch up before crossing the finish line together.

The biggest surprise came when, at the presentations that followed, I was called forward to receive a statue of a miner delicately carved in coal from the event organiser to represent Phil's memory.

Because we had ran the race with Phil's number, and deep down I knew he would have completed the run – after all the dedicated training that he had put into it – I now had to fulfil my promise to him of somehow running 100 miles!

The next few weeks proved very difficult as I completely lost all interest in my training. I had no one to ask "how is the training going?" or to follow my events. Life felt so empty. I didn't seem to care about my own health now by trying to keep ahead of the seizures. The nearest thing to training that I would achieve would be to walk across the local fields with my two faithful dogs for company.

While I was out one morning with a good friend, they suggested on visiting someone they knew who were selling some pups. Being an avid dog lover, I agreed to go along purely out of curiosity. As soon as I saw one of the pups I immediately formed a strong bond with the little fellow and before I knew it he was coming home with me. His mother was a cross between a chihuahua and a Yorkshire terrier and his father was a papillon. He was so small and would comfortably sit in the palm of my hand like a tiny bear. So I called him Paddington or Paddo for short.

In the back of my mind I kept remembering the promise that I made to Phil about running 100 miles, but all my motivation had been lost now and the thought of running a single mile didn't interest me at all. I knew I had to do something soon otherwise the seizures would return with vengeance, so I made the decision to ring Jane, who I had run the Norton half with, and ask if I could run with a group that she trained with. She told me to come along to a run on the following Monday evening at 7pm sharp to join them all for a short trail run.

When I arrived at Shepton Mallet outside a local pub, I was made to feel really welcome by the Mendip Hill Hash House Harriers (MH4 as they are also known). It was a very friendly and interesting run following a pre-laid flour trail. The faster runners would work out the correct trail to follow, while the others would follow behind, so it catered for all speeds and abilities. This was perfect for me at the time because I didn't feel as though I had to run beyond my capabilities.

Each week on a Monday evening I would look forward to running with such a friendly group. I gradually regained my interest in running and also became a lot faster and confident with it.

A few weeks later I was invited to join the Wells City Harriers running club on a Wednesday evening along with others that I got to know from the MH4 group.

Training twice a week with the groups really improved my incentive to run again and soon I joined them on a Sunday morning, often running different sections of the local Mendip Hills which greatly increased my stamina.

I had always enjoyed running the Bristol half marathon and was desperate to beat the two-hour barrier that had been so close in the past, so I entered it once again believing that I could achieve my goal.

On the morning of the race I felt so nervous. I had never felt this way before, even though each time I had previously ran to the best of my ability, I didn't feel any personal pressure.

My heart was pounding like never before as I crossed the start line with thousands of other runners all checking their watches as they started off. The crowds gave amazing support along the entire route which makes a huge difference to those taking part, especially when you are feeling at your weakest point during a run. I would pick out runners in the distance and use them as my next target to catch up with and hopefully pass. This I would do frequently throughout the race and try not to get too disillusioned by the runners that frequently passed me by.

Soon I could hear the voice of the distant commentator and began to concentrate on a fast final push to the finish line. With the sweat now pouring from my brow, I gave every ounce of strength I had on the last one hundred metres to cross the finish line.

Gasping for breath, I hung from one of the safety barriers and slowly turned around to look at the timing clock which confirmed that I had finished in 1h-46 minutes. I felt so happy to have finally smashed the elusive two-hour barrier! There was a sudden pat on my shoulder; on looking up I saw a couple of runners from our Wells running club who shook my hand and passed on their congratulations. I couldn't thank them enough for all their support on the day and for helping me with my training over the last few months.

***

Another race that I re-entered was the Snowdonia marathon. I wanted to prove to myself in some crazy way that I could run it far better on my second attempt.

I felt very apprehensive about visiting Llanberris again and didn't know if I had made the right decision, whether it was the thought of how hard it had been last time or knowing that I was now missing a major part of myself with the loss of both Steve and Phil. The evening was dark and damp when I arrived in Snowdonia and I felt utterly exhausted after finishing work and driving up. Once again, I didn't bother to erect the tent, I simply folded down the seats and after a quick take-away meal, slept in the car. As morning broke it was a bright sunny day, as I quietly sat and admired it while drinking a fresh brew of tea on the top of a huge boulder overlooking the lake.

This time the atmosphere of the run was different. I had no phone calls in the morning from Phil, which made me feel slightly insecure and lonely. It didn't matter how much I tried to remove this feeling, it remained and continued to worry me.

After talking to as many people as I could on the approach to the start line, I started to feel a little more comfortable with myself.

The race didn't feel any easier at all, even though I now knew the course route and the surprise hill near the finish. I ran as hard as I could, rewarding myself with all the magnificent scenery that passed by. My sense of deep loss tore away at me throughout the run. Occasionally I would find tears streaming down my face for no apparent reason. I was so relieved to cross the finish line and be greeted by all the spectators. I proceeded to collect my bag and got changed immediately. This time I could still walk and although my legs hurt, it was nothing compared to my first attempt.

After a few cups of tea and enough cake to fuel myself for the journey home, I was glad to be heading back to the West Country and leave all the lonely memories back behind me. It felt so good to arrive back home with my three dogs for company. I checked the race results to find I had run Snowdonia this time in 3h-57 minutes! Last year it was 4h-48 minutes, I hadn't realised just how angry I must have been this time around. The most positive part of this run was the fact that I managed to raise another £545 for the CHSW charity.

ULTRA AMBITIONS

In 2007 CHSW opened its doors at Charlton Farm in Wraxall for the very first time to care for children, who sadly are not expected to live into adulthood, and their families.

When I informed them that I had raised some more funding for them they invited me to visit their new hospice and meet the staff.

While on my tour of the building I couldn't help but notice how much work and thought had gone into this new hospice and the care that it provided to so many.

When I handed my sponsorship over to the fundraising team, I mentioned to them about the Snowdonia marathon. They all commented on running such a long distance over a difficult route. It was then that I told them about how I had made the promise to Phil of running 100 miles, to which there was total silence. With everyone focused on me – as to whether I was going to add a punchline or say that I was only kidding – came the reply "you are serious, aren't you?". "Totally" I replied. "I've made the promise and now I have to find a suitable route to run".

After thanking me again for all the sponsorship money raised, I was told to keep them informed of any plans I might have for the future in which they may be able to help. On leaving I noticed a large poster displaying the first hospice that CHSW opened in 1995 down in Fremington, near Barnstaple, and quickly asked if they knew how far away it was in terms of mileage. They said that they didn't know off hand but would look into it and let me know.

Later that evening at home I had a phone call from the fund-raising team stating that the distance between Little Bridge hospice and Charlton Farm was approximately 100 miles. I quickly enquired, "Has anyone ever walked or ran between the two establishments before?"

"Not as far as we are aware of, no".

A whole new sense of excitement now filled me. If I could run all the way between both hospices, that would fulfil my promise to Phil and raise a spectacular amount of awareness for CHSW.

I told them that I would think the new idea over and give them a call back in the near future.

I immediately found my road atlas and began planning a route that would take me from Barnstaple to Bristol. I didn't want to use the main roads as they would be far too busy with traffic, and be far too dangerous. So I opted to use quieter B roads and country lanes and soon had a route which looked really promising.

That weekend, I drove into Bath and found a stationery shop that sold every O/S map that I needed to cover the entire run, and then proceeded to mark out my intended route across each one.

After being fully satisfied with the new route, I decided to ring Charlton Farm and explain that the run, as far I could tell, was achievable and that I would be interested in making it my new goal for 2009.

With all the excitement regarding my new target for 2009 I began to increase my training. I especially enjoyed exploring new paths on the Mendip Hills and seeing the breathtaking views. By running various off-road trails I came across so many magnificent sights that I would have never have seen otherwise. It became noticeable how different the countryside would look during each of the seasons. I especially enjoyed autumn when all the leaves would change into an array of yellows, reds and gold, completely transforming the landscape.

Sometimes I would wake up in the middle of the night and reflect on the new 100 mile run that I had planned and question. Did I really think that I could run for 100 miles? The furthest I had ever done to date was an ordinary marathon. In 2007, very few people actually ran anywhere near 100 miles, now there are a lot of events covering that distance.

Sometimes, reflecting on how I had felt at the end of the previous marathons, painful memories would come back and haunt me. Surely if I took it slower, I could run for longer? But there again, how long could I possibly run for? I would need food and drinks to keep me going!

I decided to look for my first ultramarathon to run, so that I could at least answer some of the many questions that I tormented myself with.

After searching through the few ultramarathons that I could find, I came across the Thames Path Ultra, which covered 50 miles all the way from Reading back to Shepperton, Surrey.

On January 19th 2008, I drove through the early hours of the morning to arrive at Shepperton, where I parked and got on a coach to the start line at Reading.

It had poured with rain non-stop all through the night and I noticed on my journey that several places were on the verge of flooding.

On leaving the coach in Reading it was still raining heavily with huge gusts of wind that would nearly sweep you off your feet.

I couldn't help but notice there were some really serious looking runners on the start line. This was my first ultra-run and I had never met or known anyone at that time who had run 50 miles.

I just had an ordinary jacket, shorts and trainers along with my haversack that I used to carry my old school books in, while others were head to toe in Lycra, full leggings, expensive looking jackets, gloves and with trendy looking backpacks. These backpacks, the like of which I had never seen before, had pipes that fed fluids directly from the back! I had a snack box complete with a bottle of squash to accompany my oilskin leggings, that had been neatly folded and held in place by an elastic band around a little hand-held torch.

I began to feel really out of place and wondered if I had entered into something way beyond my capabilities.

After a short briefing – in which I stood at the back, out of sight with my route map firmly clenched in my hand protected from the elements in a plastic bag – we were on our way. Following the Thames Path, this was to be the start of my ultra-running experiences.

The rain continued to fall persistently. When we ran through more sheltered areas I felt so much warmer away from the cold icy wind that lashed against my exposed legs and face.

In places the Thames had flooded over the adjoining banks and we were waist deep in water trying to keep to the original paths, otherwise we would have to go miles out of the way to seek an alternative route.

While some competitors cursed out loudly as they encountered the icy cold waters, myself and a few others couldn't help but laugh our way through the murky depths.

About halfway around the circuit, with cold fingers I managed to fumble open the buckles on the haversack. It felt so good to indulge in a huge cheese sandwich and bottle of squash. With each bite I could feel how cold my hands were as they brushed against my warm face.

At this point the main group of runners had separated into several groups. I managed to find a few that I could keep up with and had good local knowledge of where the path went, even though sections of it had become engulfed with the advancing flood water.

I really enjoyed the run despite the atrocious weather conditions. I had good company, and although the miles at times seemed never ending I felt comfortable with the pace.

We finished just as it was starting to get dark in Shepperton, in a time of 9 hours-26 minutes which I was really pleased with. After thanking the fellow runners who had been so helpful to me throughout the entire route along with the race organisers, I collected my special medal and began the long, contented journey back home.

I now enjoyed the idea of taking on longer distance runs and all the challenges that came with them. When people started to ask me "how do you manage to run such long distances?" I would find a whole new sense of excitement that I had never felt before.

Looking back on my very first half marathon, having told myself that I would never go through such endurance and pain ever again seemed so far away now.

The longer distances also meant that most of my seizures had all but vanished, with overnight rest becoming something I could look forward to again.

After several more meetings with the CHSW fundraising team, we began to finalise all the plans for my 110-mile run from Barnstaple to Bristol (this worked out as the final mileage after updating all the safest and most practical routes for us to use). I drove the route – I had spent hours planning across eight different maps – over the course of many weekends to familiarise myself with it. I found toilets that would be available, not only for myself, but for the support crews, as well as places for food and shelter in case the weather took a turn for the worst.

The next thing for me to plan was an achievable timetable. Even though I had never run anywhere near this distance before.

In August, I decided to enter another 53-mile ultramarathon in Marshside, Kent, to gain more experience.

After finishing work on the Friday night, I made several flasks of hot coffee along with a variety of bread rolls and bars of chocolate, and set off overnight on the long 200-mile journey to Kent.

My sat-nav guided me through what seemed like never ending narrow country lanes before arriving at my destination outside the Gate Inn pub in Marshside. I decided to quickly snatch a few hours sleep in the comfort of the car before I woke to a beautiful morning with clear skies and complete silence apart from the birds singing.

I walked along a country lane leading away from the Inn with a fresh hot coffee steaming into the crisp morning air. After walking for a short distance, I felt relieved that all the stiffness from spending most of the night in the car had now disappeared. Just up the road a little bit further on, I spotted a field where cars full of runners were beginning to park and assemble for the race.

While attaching my race number to my shirt I could hear my phone ringing. During the few seconds that passed before I answered the call a whole range of thoughts ran through my mind. My immediate thoughts were that it was from Phil, but then the grim reality set in that he was sadly no longer with me.

On answering the call I was suddenly greeted by Ali Vowles from Radio Bristol who – after hearing about my latest adventure for CHSW – wanted to wish me good luck before going live on air at 6am. I couldn't thank her enough for her support and quickly reminded her that it was all her fault that I was running 54 miles after accepting me in her team to run the Bristol half marathon back in 2004, which gave me the running bug.

At exactly 6am, after a quick briefing, the race was started from outside the Gate Inn. We all set off, up through the secluded country lanes for the first of eight circuits around the local countryside.

As each circuit was completed, I found they became harder and harder to conquer psychologically. Not only was the day getting rapidly warmer with a beautiful cloudless sky, but after completing each circuit you couldn't help but notice that the grounds of the pub were rapidly filling with crowds of people all cheering you on with refreshing cool drinks held in their hands. Worst of all for me was the constant waft of steak simmering away on the barbeque.

I saw so many competitors giving in to the temptations of the pub, especially in the main heat of the day when the thought of competing just one more circuit proved far too much to handle. This is when I had to really focus my thoughts. I would remember the charity and sponsorship that I represented along with all the great messages and support from everyone.

Soon the friendly marshal reminded me I was on my last circuit, as I passed the pub for the final lap. With each familiar landmark I reminded myself that this was the last time I would be passing by and rewarded myself with these thoughts until I had actually finished in a time of 10hours-8 minutes.

The relief I felt on crossing the finish line was immense, as I reminded myself that this was the furthest distance I had ever run before. A neat little medal was presented to me along with a firm handshake from the race organiser and so many welcome smiles from everyone around.

From the comfort of the pub beer garden I sat casually watching the remaining runners cross the finish line, as I drank a pint of ice-cold beer. The expression on their faces said it all as they exchanged a look of desperation and pain for one of contentment and satisfaction.

By completing the run in Kent my confidence grew dramatically, particularly with all the tremendous support that I had been given. In total this run raised £1,920 for the CHSW charity which was far beyond my expectation.

A month later I ran the Bristol half marathon again. I didn't find it any easier at the time, but was absolutely delighted to find my finish time was 1h-38 minutes.

With the long runs came a whole new sense of excitement and determination to compete. I now felt far healthier than I had done for years, and even more importantly I learnt how to control the seizures which the longer running distances seemed to keep at bay.

As part of my new training technique I would experiment by sometimes running without food and drink for longer intervals, to see what effect this would have and to know what signs to look out for if I ever felt those symptoms.

Another technique that I learnt to master – which at first I thought would be impossible – was eating food while running, in order to save valuable time.

Fatigue would prove to be my worst enemy while out on my ultra-runs. I would try to distract myself from the event and what it entailed, which proved very difficult when you are on a tight schedule.

The best method I found was complete distraction from times and schedules. I would reward myself as I passed various landmarks taking in the full beauty of the surrounding countryside, thinking aloud that I would have never seen such amazing sights, had I not been out running.

At times it almost felt as if I had a little demon sat on one shoulder and an angel on the other. The demon would constantly feed me all the negative thoughts like: "What are you doing out running at this time of the night, absolutely freezing cold, when you could be wrapped up warm and resting in a nice warm bed?", to which the angel would reply: "Because you want to be a good ultra-runner you are doing the right thing. Just look at how fit and healthy you are now while raising a lot of money and awareness for charity."

For each negative thought a positive one would quickly overwhelm and replace it, fuelling me with an even stronger sense of determination.

Another major problem I found with running the longer distances was having the time to do so. I was still working anything from 55-60 hours a week, which at times left me feeling exhausted, as well as taking care of running my home on my own. But the new sense of excitement I had gained from the ultras kept me positive even through the most strenuous of times.

In order to have vital meetings with the CHSW team and discuss the intended route of 110 miles I would book days off from work.

By running with both the Wells City Harriers and MH4 clubs, I had gained so much confidence from all their help, support and guidance. I would never have been able to accomplish all the goals that I had achieved without their belief in me. I would have given up, especially after the loss of my cousin, Phil.

Bob Powell, who ran with both clubs, has had a particularly strong influence on me. He believed in every event that I did and trained me to run for enjoyment and competition, respecting others whatever their running capabilities.

Bob became my event manager and kindly co-ordinated all my timetables, routes and schedules for support, giving his own free time to do so.

We decided to arrange and finalise a date for the big run on April 29th and 30th, to commemorate the 2nd anniversary of the Charlton Farm Hospice being opened.

Now I had a fixed date in which to finalise all my training, I realised that there were only four months left until the big event. Every evening after work I would look through the selection of maps that now permanently lived on my dining room table, and study every one of the ten sections that made up the route, so that I knew them completely by memory.

So far, the longest distance that I had run was the 53 mile ultra in Kent, but I now needed to do a much longer run in order to gain vital experience.

Looking through the maps one evening, I decided that if I could incorporate some of the route I would be running in April as part of my training then this would make the run a lot more familiar – especially if I included one of the hardest sections, the long steep climb off the Somerset Levels and back up over the Mendip Hills. After many hours of planning I decided a route. From the top of the Mendip Hills I would run down into Wells, Glastonbury, Street and High Ham, then turn around at the church in West Monkton, before leaving Taunton to run the return journey back, which would cover 72 miles.

With it now being December I knew that I had a week's holiday between Christmas and the New Year, so I decided I would start my training run on Saturday 27th December. This would give me time to recover, and also if anyone wanted to join me for a section to run off some of their Christmas indulgence, they could while they were still on holiday.

I well remember on Saturday 27th December, 2008, driving into the Castle of Comfort car park at 1-45am. The pub is situated right on the top of the Mendip Hills between the villages of East Harptree and Priddy. It was a beautiful moonlit night with a sky just full of amazing stars that sparkled like jewels above me.

While waiting to meet a couple of other runners who were starting off with me at 2am, I had enough time to sort out my backpack and make sure that I had enough spare clothing and food for the day.

As I opened the car door I instantly felt a rush of freezing cold air, sending a chill throughout my entire body. The temperature in the car recorded -2C as the demon on my shoulder reminded me that it wasn't too late to pull out of this run. Just as a positive thought pushed this to one side I saw the headlights from my support runners car fast approaching through the darkness of the night.

Donning hats, scarves, and several layers of clothing I left the freezing car park along with Tracey, Jane and James, as we quickly set off up the road towards the shining red lights in the distance of Penn Hill television mast.

We hadn't got 50 metres from the car park when we saw a car's headlights cautiously approaching us. As it slowly drew closer, we could see it was a police patrol car. The passenger window slowly slid open and I could instantly feel the warm air escape from within. A stern voice enquired "And what are you lot up to?" I replied that we were on a charity awareness run about to cover 72 miles, to which he said "You must be mad! Just go careful as its very icy out there", before slowly disappearing back into the night.

From the light of our torches, the road and hedgerows glistened and sparkled in a multitude of colours. Apart from the occasional owl protesting in the distance, all you could hear was the sound of our footsteps in this truly magical landscape.

The streets of Wells were totally deserted. Apart from ourselves there wasn't a single soul to be seen. No pedestrians, no cars, just total silence illuminated by the Christmas lights that gently swung overhead in the clutches of a shallow breeze.

This was to be my very first experience of running throughout the night. I quickly found that I loved the idea of running without the hustle and bustle of everyday traffic, through crowds of people and found great comfort from it.

On approaching Glastonbury High Street the fresh night air soon began to fill with the delicious smell of freshly cooked bread which had us all feeling pretty hungry. Slowly, one by one, we could hear the first voices, as the sun began to break through the night sky, taking with it each star in turn, as the first golden rays of light began to sparkle and pierce their way into the new day.

The support runners that came to join me from both Wells City Harriers (WCH) and MH4 were amazing. Throughout the day and without fail they would happily join me on my six-stage journey. At one point very early in the morning, Radio Somerset rang me for a live interview. I described to listeners how beautiful the Somerset Levels looked on this cold and frosty morning. Soon afterwards, random cars would blow their horns and wave to us, as we passed through several tiny villages on the approach to Taunton.

In the distance, on one of the main road sections, we could see a car that had pulled into a lay-by ahead of us. I presumed it was one of our support runners who had come out to join us, but instead it was a Radio Somerset listener. She had heard my story earlier and very kindly brought me warm mince pies, along with refreshing hot coffee. I couldn't thank her enough for her support and had to be told several times by my support runners to slow down over the following few miles, as they couldn't keep up with me after my sudden uplift, gained through somebody elses kindness.

As this was my first planned ultra-run, using my own schedule and route, the time passed very quickly. I found myself constantly checking the laminated schedule that I carried with me throughout the duration of the day.

Instead of thinking in a negative manner about how far I still had to go, I remembered to reward myself again with each location gained from the schedule. Late into the afternoon, I had beaten my previous record of non-stop running by completing 11 hours. Fatigue was now beginning to show, with a sense of tiredness that I had never experienced before. This demanded extra concentration to maintain a pace and keep on schedule.

Slowly but surely, into the fast approaching night sky, one by one the stars began to reappear. Multiplying by the minute, until they filled the whole atmosphere above us with mesmerising shapes and patterns.

Climbing the last few miles, up through steep country lanes that led to the top of the Mendips, proved really demanding. My body now complained and ached as never before. It was so tempting and easy to give up at this point, and just climb into the warm support car that followed us.

Removing my cap swiftly from my head, I gave it a very quick slap over my left shoulder, as if to remove the demon that had been tormenting me. One of my support runners asked if I was okay to which I replied that I just getting rid of any doubts I was having. Sharing positive thoughts with my angel, I quickly accomplished the last few miles of the run. On the approach back to the Castle of Comfort, from where I had started some 17 hours earlier, there were supporters lighting up both sides of the road to welcome me home.

Soon I was settled in the pub with a mug of hot tea grasped firmly in both hands and a large log fire driving out the last of the night's chill from within my bones. It had been a fantastic and emotional journey, achieving my greatest mileage to date through everyone's incredible support. But one serious thought kept emerging from the back of my mind: what I didn't show through all my smiles that evening was the fact that in order to complete my run in just four months time, I would have to run another half of what I had run that day, on top of what I had just accomplished.

WOBBLY WEEKEND TRAINING SESSIONS

With the countdown to 29th April and the 110-mile run now fast approaching, I managed to enter a couple of long trail running events to try and maintain a decent level of fitness. I decided that trail running required a higher level of stamina than road running because of the constant changes over strenuous terrain. It also presented less impact on my joints compared with running on roads and lanes.

In February 2009, I wrote the following story for a website that a colleague of mine, Martin, so kindly set up for me.

***

The start of the Butleigh race saw 70 runners line up for the seven-mile multi terrain run. During the first mile I could still feel the effects of the previous weekend's 20-mile Grizzly run pulling on me. It didn't help with me running a seven-minute first mile, especially as I had just run 21 miles to attend this event.

As I ran up one of the hills overlooking Butleigh, I started to struggle to maintain my position. Not wanting anyone to overtake, I pressed on as hard as I could. No matter how hard I tried I could hear footsteps behind me. I tried desperately to escape them as they followed me like a shadow.

It felt really good to cross the finish line, but now was not the time to hang around. I had noticed before the race all of the delicious homemade cakes on offer and a lot of runners had been in front of me during the event!

Now was the time to head back for the hills. I had to run the 21-

mile route back home over the Mendip Hills to Westfield.

My feet felt sore as I changed back into road shoes. The whole idea of combining all three runs was to get used to running while both sore and tired. This was only a taste of things to come if I was to complete the 110-mile run in April.

Previously on my run down to Butleigh a whole box of flapjacks had disappeared. So to compensate on the journey home a good selection of homemade cakes was my insurance.

Eleven miles out from Butleigh at the base of the Mendip Hills, I knew I was in trouble and my legs were really struggling. Just keeping going and focusing took every grain of strength both physically and mentally. I became my own worst enemy at this point. One half of me, the demon, just wanted to sit down and have a break, while the other half, the angel, kept reminding me about the 'little' run I had planned in April and how it was going to be a damn sight harder than what I was experiencing now. I told myself to stop whinging and to get my useless body up over the Mendips!

Thinking positive is crucial. I started thinking about all the other times that I had run up over the Mendips in the past and began to question why I was finding it so difficult now.

After struggling for another two miles I felt ready to call it a day. Had this one training session really beaten me? Had I taken on far more than I anticipated? Had the previous week's training been too much for me to do this run without a break?

As I passed a bus stop, the temptation proved too much to resist, so I sneaked in to read the timetable. There was a bus due in only eight minutes. I could see the demon on my shoulder, rubbing his hands with a huge smile. The angel's reaction, with her arms folded tightly, is unprintable! So slowly I placed one foot in front of the other and made my way up the hill, while all the time waiting for the bus to pass by.

Looking back over my shoulder at the views over Glastonbury and Wells I could see that I had nearly conquered the Mendips.

I now had only seven more miles to go. While passing a lay-by, a car drove in and stopped. The driver, an elderly gentleman, eagerly enquired as to where I was going. I told him "Westfield", to which he replied "So am I. Jump in". This was so tempting! I had every excuse to do just this, as every part of me really hurt. It would have been the most sensible decision to have made. The trouble with me, though, is that I don't like sensible, especially when on a mission to achieve a personal goal.

As I watched the car disappear into the distance, I reminded myself that I only had five more miles to go until I reached home, and told myself to "Get moving, otherwise it would soon be dark and you've still got the chickens to feed!"

I don't know who was more pleased to see me at my front door: myself or my three dogs, who started licking me to death. The feeling of reaching my personal goal was worth every bit of the struggle and pain in my legs.

***

As the alarm clock rattled away for what seemed like an eternity I finally managed to silence it by knocking it off the bedside cabinet.

Trying to convince myself how important it was to get to the training session at Cheddar that morning, and not have another warm hour in bed, I tried to ignore how frosty it looked outside. The first problem I came across was how to get into my car, which had frozen solid overnight.

As I drove across the top of the Mendip Hills that morning, the roads were treacherous, with black ice covering many sections.

Six of us set off from the Kings of Wessex School in Cheddar, straight up over the steep side of the gorge. After about a mile my pockets were filled with my discarded gloves and thermal hat. Another half a mile further on saw my top and another layer removed. Slightly overdressed!

We eventually stopped very briefly at the top of the gorge to catch our breath. Looking around at the surrounding views, everything was frozen solid and capped in a thick layer of frost – a totally different landscape to that which we had seen before.

It felt good to be out training, burning off the excess dinners, Christmas cake, puddings and pies. Anyway I could think this way now because the hard work had been done and we were on a roll back down from the top of the gorge. It would be downhill all the way now until we reached the car park at the bottom where we had started.

Another good run finished over unfamiliar footpaths and frosty landscapes. Looking over at my discarded trainers steaming away on the frosty car park floor, I realised how lucky I was to have a running group on a Sunday morning and be part of a good team.

***

As I left home on a Saturday morning for another trail run, it was absolutely pouring down with rain. While sat in the car it sounded like I had a mad drummer hammering away on the roof, as the huge drops of rain continued to fall. But when I arrived in Cranmore, some seven miles on, the sun came out and the skies cleared.

Six of us started off on the run and after climbing a few hills and trampling through rain-sodden fields, my legs started to feel like lead!

The dreaded flu bug had taken its toll on me again the previous weekend. With a bowl of porridge in one hand and a fist full of tissues in the other, I decided to call a halt to all the training. But this was another weekend and I wasn't going to let some nasty bugs ruin more vital training sessions. I thought to myself, surely if you don't give in, you can burn them off during a good hard training session. With this idea firmly in mind, I set off with the other runners and tried to ignore my legs, which were screaming at me!

I must have looked at every detail on Cranmore Tower as we passed, using it as a mild distraction from all the discomfort that I now felt.

Later on, during the run, we released a trapped ram that we found laying flat out on its back totally tangled up in the long thorns of a bramble hedge. By the look of it, he must have been there all night!

Ten miles had now passed and after checking everything on me was where it should be, I now felt a lot better. At least this weekend I had not given in to the dreaded bug and as a reward I had a full, no sorry *two*, full English breakfasts from the local café.

***

Another Saturday morning saw three of us taking part in a circuit training session down at Wells rugby club with our instructor, Terry, for one of his intensive workout sessions.

With the heart pounding, sweat dripping and aching muscles – that I didn't even know I owned – we worked our way through his training regime. While we were on our backs, arms and legs pointing towards the heavens, I noticed a lady trying to park her car and completely getting it wrong. She had obviously seen us all on the floor doing what must have looked like a dying fly act!

In the afternoon I decided to look around a large bike shop in Yeovil. Not having bought a bike without an engine for 20-something years, this was going to prove a real experience.

The reason for a bike? I decided that I needed more hours training if I was to run non-stop for 27 hours, and I didn't want to inflict too much impact on my poor joints. I certainly couldn't swim anywhere near the hours needed. I felt as though I had nearly drowned the previous week after just two hours!

So I decided cycling would be the answer that I was looking for and chose a triathlon bike, because the frame is designed to hold you as near to the running position as possible.

I came out of the shop with a bike that resembled something you might find in a Star Wars movie. The handlebars were totally different to what I had come across before, with no room for a large basket – so Paddo would be disappointed – and cables everywhere.

Sunday morning I woke up thinking to myself: "Do I really have to drive down to the Blackmoor Vale half marathon?" It was really cold outside and I hadn't had the chance to test out my new (toy) bike yet.

Bishop's Courdle, near Sherbourne, was freezing cold with a wind that would sooner go through, rather than around, you. This was the first time in a competition run that I competed wearing jogging bottoms and a jacket as it felt so cold.

The wind was head on for the duration of the run, which made me feel very glad with my decision to wear warmer clothing. I could still feel the chill even after several hard miles of running.

With a lot of cursing under my breath, I managed to reach the top of the last hill which stretched from mile 12 to just short of the finish line.

A flask of coffee, another of soup, four hot-cross buns, a Cornish pasty and a packet of crisps soon put any signs of hunger at bay, supplying enough fuel for the journey home.

The following weekend, on Saturday morning, I wiped the sleep away from my eyes realising that it was only a few weeks until my 110-mile CHSW run.

The day started off with Terry's circuit training exercises at Millfield School, Street. It was an hour's solid training, which really made you come away with a sense of achievement, because everything on you hurts so much! It was a weird experience, sprinting on a static bike, then getting off and sprinting as hard as I could up a hill –while trying to run in a straight line. The last time I can remember my legs feeling like that was after an over indulgent Friday night up at the White Post Inn!

On the way home, while passing Glastonbury Tor, I had a bright idea. "I wonder how many people have run to the top?" Perhaps we should give it a go. I say 'we' because I had my little pup "Paddo" with me and I was sure he would enjoy a little walk.

Half an hour later we had run from the Abbey car park to the base of the Tor then proceeded on our way up. After many strange looks we arrived at the top. Paddo was first, looking back down at me from under the Tor as if to say: "What kept you, old man?"

On our way home, Paddo was rewarded with his favourite meal: sausage and chips. Five minutes later, looking over into the passenger seat, all I could see was four legs pointing towards the roof of the car.

***

The following Sunday morning saw the launch of my new bike ready for cross-training. I had used it during evenings on a static turbo-trainer but not yet on the road.

As I set off out of Westfield I found it much harder than expected as the thin hard tyres picked up a lot of vibration from the road.

About two miles up the road, I stopped in a lay-by to answer my phone. It was then that I remembered I was wearing clip on shoes, that slot into the pedals! Too late. I pulled myself out of a ditch cursing at being so stupid, as I wiped the mud and leaves off, having learnt a valuable lesson.

Later, as I approached the main traffic lights in Shepton Mallet, I tried to practice clipping out of the pedals. Despite having worked perfectly several times on the approach, they would not now release. With the lights now red I still couldn't put either foot on the floor and ended up hanging off the traffic light stem with both arms, smiling politely at the passing traffic!

Later, I met up with my friend Ian on his bike at Wraxall Hill, from where we both made our way to Yeovil and the surrounding areas. We were rewarded at Laurie and Aiden's home in Cranmore with a lovely fresh brew of tea. Having cycled 61 miles on my first road trip, I found it a great form of cross-training, but was seriously thinking of replacing the seat with an armchair.

THE LONG ROUTE HOME

With only two weeks left now until 29th April, the CHSW team were doing a fantastic job promoting the 110-mile event, which they labelled the 'Champions for Children' run.

My biggest surprise came when Olympian, European and Commonwealth long distance runner Jo Pavey announced she would join me for the start of the event. To have someone of Jo's calibre running with me was unbelievable and truly a great honour.

After a long journey to Fremington with Bob Powell, the event organiser, we arrived at Little Bridge House. Little Bridge was the first of the children's hospices to be opened by the CHSW charity.

We were immediately greeted by Eddie Farwell MBE, co-founder of CHSW, who proceeded to show us around the hospice, where we met several members of their dedicated staff.

Our aim that day was to promote the 'Champions for Children' run with the help of several radio stations including Radio Somerset, Radio Bristol and Radio Devon as well as ITV and Sky News.

A massive surprise I had that morning was meeting Jo Pavey and her husband Gavin. They had travelled over four hours and through snow to reach Little Bridge to help promote the event.

For the rest of the morning I gave press and radio interviews, which I found really hard as I had only given the occasional interview before. I couldn't believe how much attention this event was now attracting.

The main thing that I wanted to convey to the public was just how much amazing care and support the CHSW team provided, not only to the children with life-limiting conditions, but to their families as well. Most nerve-wracking I found were the interviews in front of TV cameras, which were due to be shown later that evening all over the South West region.

After meeting more of the care teams and some families, it was time for me to leave. I couldn't thank Jo and Gavin enough for the inspiration that they had given me along with everyone else I had met at Little Bridge.

As we drove out of the long driveway from the hospice, I couldn't help but think that in just 14 days time I would be leaving there and running all the way back to Bristol.

As Bob drove us back home, covering most of the route that I would be running, I had time to relax and reflect on all the day's events. This is when it suddenly dawned on me just how big this was going to be; not only physically demanding due to the crazy number of miles, but also mentally. I would have all the public watching, seeing if I could actually complete what seemed an impossible task, with the minimum amount of experience.

As I sat at home that evening with Paddo snoozing on my lap and Scooby and Bonnie lying in front of the blazing wood burner, I watched the local news promoting my run to the world. "That's it", I thought to myself, there is no backing out now, all my dreams and ambitions have gone public.

The following weekend, me and Bob met up with all the support drivers who would be escorting me for the big run. It would be a chance for them to get familiarised with the route and all of the change-over points along the ten sections, where vital food and hot drinks would be available.

In the main offices at CHSW, the staff were busy answering phonecalls, as people registered their place to join me running along various sections of the route, and generous donations were being made. Around £10,000 had now been pledged, even before the run had started.

With only two days to go, after returning home from work, I checked my two kit bags thoroughly, just hoping that I had more than enough gear to cover me for the event in all weather conditions.

I had lost count of the amount of times I studied all the maps, but at least now the route was fully memorised, I could reward myself along the way, as I passed through each and every village on the long journey back to Bristol.

Watching the sun seep its way through the tiny gap in the hotel curtains during the early morning of 29th April 2009, I felt so glad that it was good weather outside and not pouring with rain as it had done on so many of my runs.

I only managed to nap for a few hours with the incessant worrying. Had I really prepared enough to complete this run? Had I covered every eventuality that could arise over the days ahead?

The morning quickly passed as we prepared for the 1pm start. Packing all the food was a stark reminder of the task which lay before me. There were 10 bags of food, one for each section of the route.

Talking to Jo Pavey and her husband, Gavin, before the start of the run was a great reassurance to me, as was watching the support vehicles and their crews prepare to leave. All the time and effort everyone was putting into this was amazing.

After giving several interviews for the local media, it was time for me to start the run. Eddie Farwell, did the final countdown, and then suddenly it was all very real, nine months of preparation had finally come to life. As Jo and I set off along the driveway and out through the entrance gates of Little Bridge Hospice, I can remember seeing all the faces of the staff, children with their families and spectators, as a huge sense of emotion came over the pair of us.

More than 100 miles of road now lay ahead of me. No time to worry now, just enjoy and focus on the run.

As we passed the clocktower in Barnstaple we were joined by the first group of support runners. It was then that I realised we were running too fast after being caught up in all the excitement. I casually smiled to myself as I thought at this rate I would be back at home by tea-time, before bringing the pace back on track.

Jo stayed with us for several extra miles than was originally planned. I was sorry to see her go, but extremely grateful for her friendship and the support that she had given to all of us.

Food and drink had to be consumed at regular intervals, whether I felt I needed it or not. This was one crucial thing I kept reminding myself about. If I didn't get this right then there wouldn't be a finish and all my training would have been a complete waste of time.

Coming to the changeover points for the support runners, approximately every 10 miles, gave me a great boost. Each changeover marked the passing of a huge chunk of the route. I felt really grateful to all the amazing runners who had come out and encouraged me. I also looked forward to finding out what each new group would be like and enjoyed watching their reaction to the atmosphere of it all.

On one of the early stages, I can remember having a lot of banter with some of the great personnel that had come along to join us from 848 Naval Air Squadron of the Royal Navy Fleet Air Arm. They operated the Westland Sea King helicopters from RNAS Yeovilton.

There was a change to the usual food intake at one stage, as we passed through Bampton and headed out of town up a steep hill. To my surprise I was tapped on the back by the runner behind who then passed a bag of fresh hot chips over my shoulder. Glancing behind me, I could see various bags of chips being passed around, that were given to us by a very kind chip shop owner. He had seen us on the local news and after wishing us a safe run, said that he hoped it would help us on our long journey through Devon.

The roads from Barnstaple to Milverton seemed at times to climb forever. This is where all the hard training and discipline really began to pay off.

As we ran into the darkness of the evening, I felt really comfortable. The weather was good and I always enjoyed running at night. Perhaps when it is dark you concentrate a lot more on your natural senses rather than relying on just what you can see around you.

I always liked the different smells at night, especially those of fresh dew on the ground or dampness from the still night air. On several occasions we also encountered the smell of freshly mowed grass and the fragrant scent of honeysuckle in the hedgerows. The distinct noises of animals also became more apparent as we passed through the countryside at night.

The flashing beacons from the support vehicles, piercing through the darkness, proved to be a great distraction and sense of comfort as they guided us safely through the night. People now lined up outside some of the pubs in the cold night air and cheered us as we went through.

Quite unexpectedly in the remotest of areas, we would pass dustbins and gates with messages of support strapped to them, which provided a welcome boost to all taking part.

As with all my long runs, you can never tell what is going to happen. The night so far had been relatively quiet. This was about to change, as we ran along the A361 towards West Lyng, and a car drew up alongside us. The drivers window wound down and from the beam of my headtorch I could see an elderly gentleman, who shouted "ere mate, there's a wild steer running about in that road up thur". Then quickly, while winding up his window, he shouted: "And ee's got big horns as well", before hurriedly driving off in a large plume of smoke, disappearing into the darkness.

By now we had all stopped and just looked at each other before breaking out into fits of laughter. Was he serious? Or had he had one too many drinks down at the local pub?

One of the support crews decided to go ahead and check out the situation while we followed on behind. Smiling to myself, I could imagine this turning into a scene resembling the streets of Spain, with us all getting chased by a charging bull. Knowing my luck, I would probably get chased all the way back to Barnstaple!

The crew did find a steer on the road ahead, where it was guided into the safety of a nearby field and reported.

The night hours quickly passed, as the first signs of daylight calmly greeted us onto the moorlands approaching High Ham. It had now persistently rained for a good few hours and I noticed that the laces on my left trainer had rubbed against the top of my foot, causing the tendons to become very sore. I quickly slackened off the tension and thought to myself, if this was the only problem that I had after running 68 miles, for 16 hours on hard road surfaces, then I wasn't doing too bad.

This was the first of many lessons that I would learn from running ultra-distances. The longer you are out there on any running event, the more your feet will swell in your trainers. So now, instead of using ordinary laces, that are pretty unforgiving, I use elastic laces that stretch and help loosen the trainers around your feet as they expand.

As we approached Street, then Glastonbury and Wells, I felt really confident about how the run was progressing. Yes, I began to hurt, but not in a negative way. I had expected to suffer a lot more than I did at this stage, especially after remembering how I felt when I ran the 72-miles only four months earlier.

Now having run further than ever before, I had beaten my personal record and was on what I classed as home ground as I ran up through Wells High Street. It felt good to be back closer to home, after so many miles. It also brought back so many memories of Wednesday night training runs with the Wells City Harriers.

Climbing up out of Wells on the steep lanes through Milton, my legs suddenly felt really tired and unresponsive. Having covered 90 miles of the journey, I knew that I had to focus harder than ever before to achieve the next 20. I found this really hard because along with the fatigue came sleep deprivation that would, at times, engulf my whole body, making me feel like curling up into a ball and falling asleep on the side of the road.

I would have just loved to have slept anywhere. But I knew if I did I would have the near impossible task of getting going again, and lose valuable time that I had no chance of regaining.

With a fresh brew of tea firmly clasped in my hands, I briefly stopped for a while on the steep slopes of Milton Hill, trying to balance myself by leaning forwards on tired legs. The tea tasted so refreshing, but my dry mouth and throat were telling me that I didn't want anything else to eat at this stage, as I wouldn't have been able to swallow any solids.

As I painfully placed one foot in front of the other, a loud cheer along with words of encouragement came from the support runners, which helped me to regain some positivity.

I had just made the ascent to the top of the Mendips, passing Penn Hill television mast, when I recieved a call from Emma Britton of Radio Somerset. She asked if it was okay for me to say a few words to all her listeners. They'd had so many enquiries about how the run was progressing, which immediately engulfed me with a new sense of enthusiasm, knowing that so many people were following this throughout the South West region.

During the interview, I commented that when things got really tough and I felt really sore, I just had to think of the children and their families from the two hospices. I told Emma I had to remember how lucky I was to get my own health and strength back compared to how I had been five years earlier. My aches and pains today were only temporary I could put up with them. But the families I was raising money to help didn't have that choice.

About 30 minutes after the interview, I recieved a message from one of the support vehicles saying that Radio Somerset's telephone switchboard was jammed with incoming calls from listeners wishing me the best of luck and a safe journey. About a month later, I was told the interview had been nominated for an award.

The toughest of all the sections, in terms of ascent, had now been completed, but I still couldn't regain my pace as my legs felt so tight and painful. Resting against the back of one of the support vehicles, I tried to balance on one leg and grasp the other leg while pulling it up behind my back. It was so full of lactic acid that it wasn't going anywhere. Bob, who had ran sections with me and supported me along the whole event, quickly came to help. He managed, after several attempts, to release the offending acid from my legs, gently raising them, as they slowly but surely regained movement and flexibility.

Throughout the run I had to remain positive so I would reward myself by passing landmarks or achieving certain distances. The Hunters Lodge in Priddy, after climbing up over the Mendip Hills via the old Bristol Road, was one such landmark. Another was the Castle of Comfort pub on top of Smitham's Hill, East Harptree, both of which gave me an incredible welcome with crowds of supporters outside helping to make all the aches and pains briefly fade away.

After refreshments and having a new batch of support runners join me at the Castle of Comfort, the route took me down the dreaded Smitham's Hill, which lasts for two and a half miles. It felt like the longest couple of miles in my life! Running down the hill on very tender and sore legs was extremely painful to endure.

I tried running sideways to ease the pain but with each step it felt as though the top of my legs had been sliced open. To make the situation worse, where my feet had got wet from all the puddles on the roads – despite several changes of socks – huge blisters had now formed on both the bottoms of my feet and on the end of my toes.

To dismiss the pain my feet were now giving me I tried to focus on the fact that I had only 18 more miles to cover. I could then spend several days resting up and recovering in the comfort of my own home. Just 18 more miles!

As I approached East Harptree, I saw that the whole of the primary school had come out and lined the street to cheer me through. Passing by all the youngsters standing proudly with their teachers, waving bunting, flags and cheering me on like a hero, was very emotional. This helped enormously to regain my focus and lift my confidence when most needed.

On the approach to East Harptree cemetery, I collected a bouquet of flowers from my sister-in-law, Heather, then slowly walked over to the grave of my two cousins, Phil and Steve.

Gently laying the flowers made my heart sink and my eyes filled with emotion with the harsh reminder of losing both of them in just two years. But as I left through the cemetery gates, I suddenly recalled one of Phil's sarcastic remarks that he used to say to me: "Call yourself a runner?" Picturing his cheeky grin, all my sadness disappeared and was replaced with a smile.

On approaching a mini-roundabout in Chew Magna, I could see some people stood in the middle supporting a large banner. As I got closer, I could see that it marked the 100th milestone. Standing there with the biggest smile I had seen all day was my little Godson, Ryan, alongside his mother, Tracey.

I had finally fulfilled my promise to Phil and achieved my goal of a lifetime, but there was still 10 long miles remaining in order to reach the second hospice in Wraxall.

The final changeover point for the support runners took part outside the Prince of Waterloo pub in Winford. At each of the ten changeover positions, I had been weighed on a set of scales to keep an eye on hydration levels. I found that all the way through, I had slightly gained weight. I personally blame the chips I ate back in Bampton!

The last doughnut had now been shared with a fellow runner and tasted as good as the first, even though it had survived 102 miles. My phone rang again and to my delight it was Jo Pavey, wishing me good luck for the finish and congratulating me on all the miles covered. This was a huge boost to my morale and one of the memories that I shall never forget.

Tyntesfield estate was a fabulous sight, with the end of the run now within reach. But my feet were now in a terrible state. Across the whole of the bottom of each foot stretched one very painful blister, from my toes all the way back to the far end of each ankle.

Each step now taken felt really painful, as I could feel the fluid inside move from the front to the back of my feet. Then the pain intensified as the huge blisters began to break down and leak into my trainers. It felt as though I was walking barefoot across broken glass. Trying as best as I could to keep smiling and block out all the pain, I concentrated every ounce of thought on finishing the final two miles. It didn't matter that it was freezing cold, getting dark and pouring down with rain, we were nearly there at the elusive finish.

It was a long and steep climb up the hill leading out of the grand Tyntesfield estate, but a really beautiful one, as it led through tree-lined avenues that helped shelter us from the storm.

I suddenly noticed for the first time during the whole event that all the runners were completely silent. It was as if we had all been overcome by some magical spell. Now was the time to reflect on what we had actually achieved: 109 miles with only one more mile to go!

While running along the busy main road, I noticed on the entrance to the estate a large circle formed in flour with a hook going through its centre. As a member of the MH4 running group, I knew this was a fish hook, and the first runner to pass it had to double back behind the entire group to join the last runner. With a huge smile I decided to break the rules on this occasion and continued leading the runners into the estate. With Charlton Farm now in sight and Bob, Jane, Pat, Carol and Nicola to accompany me, we made our way down the long tarmac road which led towards the cheering crowds that had gathered to see us finish.

The sky was now dark and angry from the storm, as our support vehicles helped light up the final section of road before us with their headlamps. Passing through the green tape marking the 110-mile finish line to the welcome of all the supporters was truly an unforgettable experience.

Looking around me I saw amongst the crowd three of the families that stay at the hospice, which was very emotional. Seeing their smiles was worth every step taken.

Having crossed the finish line, I felt as though it wasn't just me who had achieved this amazing goal, it was down to the perfect team work: the support vehicle crews, support runners, spectators (who had come out to cheer us in all weather conditions), the people who had donated money, plus everyone at home who followed my progress and silently wished me a safe journey.

CHILLED TO THE BONE

After completing the 110-mile route, I felt so pleased that the event had attracted so much awareness for the CHSW charity, along with a phenomenal £20,000 in donations, which rose to £25,000 over the following months.

I had fulfilled my promise to Phil by completing the 100-mile challenge and come so far with my running in just over five years, but I still wasn't happy with myself. I was tormented and deep inside I felt that I could have done far better than I did.

Looking back over photographs of the run, I would feel uncomfortable about how bad I looked. There was also the fact that I was advised to go to hospital to have checks after briefly passing out half an hour after I had finished, which only added to my doubts.

Several weeks after the run my feet had completely healed back to their original state. They had been in such a terrible and painful mess after the event that I did wonder if they would ever fully recover.

Amongst all the great messages of support that I had received, as always I did get some negative comments. I was told by one person, who I thought I knew quite well, that I only picked the pretty runs like Snowdonia and Windermere, instead of taking on real fell running trails, while others sarcastically told me it was time to give it all up, as I was too old!

Although I can't deny these comments did hurt, I refused to show it externally. Inside I was savage and thought how dare they. What had they achieved in life? They hadn't a clue what I had come through, or how much I had put into the last five years.

Another problem I had to overcome was the sense of feeling lost. So much planning and organisation had gone into the 110-mile event that I was beginning to miss all that. Along with the loss of my cousins, everything felt so quiet and I started to feel a strange emptiness creeping in.

A month later I received a surprise, when all the support crews and some of the representatives from CHSW all got together and invited me to celebrate the run with an evening out in Tiverton.

Just as we were about to sit down for a meal, we were joined by Jo Pavey and Gavin. This was a huge honour for me, especially when I was presented with a large picture frame, filled with photographs from the event.

While at work one afternoon in July, I received a phone call from the CHSW charity asking if I was available to visit Charlton Farm the following week.

I was keenly met a week later by several staff at the reception of Charlton Farm, who seemed excited as to what was about to happen.

They explained that they had a special surprise awaiting me as we all proceeded to walk across the car park in the direction of some large empty fields. It was then that I could hear the distinct noise of a helicopter approaching. Gazing up into the clear blue sky, I could see it circling several times before landing in the fields next to us. As the aircraft settled down the side door flew open and out jumped several members of 848 Squadron RNAS Yeovilton who had joined me on the 110-mile run.

I was greeted by loud cheers, huge hugs and a lot of banter from the lads who had just returned to Yeovilton on leave. In their own time they had flown up with a cheque for £500 to present to the hospice. I just stood there in complete amazement and couldn't believe the kindness and generosity of these men. We then proceeded to the hospice, where they asked if they could have a tour and see the amazing work that was being done there.

Later, after the tour, the crew enquired if any of the children or their families would like to look around their helicopter. Minutes later the families were greatly entertained as they explored the huge Sea King aircraft.

After the cheque presentation and giving several of the children various toys, it was time for the crew to leave. Before departing, they kindly told me that if I needed any other support on an event, they would gladly join me once again, if they were available.

As the helicopter circled once more before disappearing from sight, I felt a huge amount of pride just knowing these incredible young men.

***

For the next couple of months, I kept up all my regular training with both the Wells and MH4 running groups, doing short runs mainly around the Mendip Hills.

Although I was still occupied working long hours, catching up on jobs around the home and training, I still carried a sense of emptiness that seemed to haunt me from within.

On several occasions I would automatically try to ring Steve or Phil, before the reality would suddenly hit me that they were no longer here.

Slowly but surely the seizures that I had experienced, before my long run, gradually began to invade my body once more. At first, I just tried to ignore them and hope that they would go away, but the stark reality was that they were here to stay unless I did something about it.

After several blood tests and various other hospital examinations, the fact remained that I either had to control my body through a training regime or I simply went back on strong medication.

Medication to me was simply out of the question, I wanted to remain totally in control of my body. I had been so lucky up to now to find that running enabled me to do so.

After several evenings of arguing with myself about what I was going to do to maintain my future fitness, I decided that I would take on an even longer run.

This would either end as a total disaster or it would settle the continuous torment that I had been carrying ever since the dreadful finish of my 110-mile run.

For hours, with my dogs sat either side of me, I would sit and contemplate in total silence, juggling all the pros and cons associated with doing another long run. Occasionally when I was satisfied with a decision, I would share it with them, to which they would peer up at me in a fixed gaze and excitably beat the sofa with their tails.

CHSW announced new plans to build a third hospice in St Austell to cater for families in the Plymouth and Cornwall regions. I thought this would be the perfect opportunity for me to represent them again if I could do another run covering that area. The CHSW 'Champions for Children' logo would remain fresh in the minds of others and I could help bring in vital funding for the building of their new hospice.

Although my seizures were reappearing rapidly now – I would get out of bed as many as four times in a single night – I classed myself as being lucky, as I could remove the pain by walking around for 15 minutes. Sometimes I would curse intently and ask "why me?" Then I would remember the families I had seen while I was in hospital. I knew they were in a far worse condition than myself and I would suddenly feel really selfish for complaining. This would then make me refocus on what had to be done in order to raise more vital funding for them.

Staring at Bob over the top of a large mug of tea – using it as if it was some kind of safety shield – I slowly explained to him about my plans for an even longer run which I wanted to do early the following year.

Bob had not only coached me with the Wells running club, he had taught me so many things about running. But most importantly he believed in me and supported me on all my big events.

There was a long pause of silence as I awaited Bob's verdict about my latest crazy idea, followed by a huge smile (and some unprintable language), to which I felt so much relief.

For several evenings at home I endlessly studied a large road atlas and decided, as the new children's hospice was going to be built in Cornwall, serving the county and also Plymouth, what better place to start the run than on Plymouth Hoe and finish back in Westfield.

I explained my plans to Bob over several more cups of tea. The final route that I came up with covered 140 miles. Starting at Plymouth, the run would take me over Dartmoor, through Exeter, cover the range of the Blackdown Hills, then join the Somerset Levels before finally climbing the Mendip Hills to finish at Radstock.

Bob, shaking his head, looked up from the maps and peered directly at me with the question: "Do you think you can do it?" I replied immediately that I could, stating that I would make damn sure that it would be a far better finish than my last one, to which we both chuckled and shook hands.

Bob's opinion meant everything to me, all his training and support had given me a new outlook on life and showed me what could be achieved if you truly believe in yourself.

The fundraising team were amazed and delighted to have our new challenge promoting them once again. The final figure raised from the 110-mile run had now just exceeded £25,000, which was a phenomenal amount of money and far beyond any expectations that I had ever envisaged.

To help contain the seizures I increased my long runs every weekend. I would cover 30 mile trail routes over the Mendips, admiring all the stunning views that changed with each season.

By now I had become so familiar with all the local trails that there was very little need for a map. This meant hardly any planning as I made each trail up as I ran.

While out on long runs, I always wore the 'Champions for Children' logo, along with a Union Jack flag that flew from a standard attached to my backpack. People who regularly recognised the flag would know that it was me and the reasons for doing so.

My next competition run was the Bristol half marathon, which I thoroughly enjoyed. I couldn't believe it when I gained the unbelievable time of 1h-31 minutes, a time that I never could have envisaged a few years previously.

One week later, Martin, who had done a fantastic job organising a website for me to place all my weekly postings on, organised the first Uphill to Wells relay race. This was a 30 mile route divided into six stages, where competitors would hand over a baton to the next runner in their team, as they covered the entire length of the West Mendip Way, across the Mendip Hills.

The race would start on the beach at Uphill, about a mile from Weston-super-Mare. It would incorporate a steep ascent onto the Mendip Hills, offering fabulous views from Crook Peak, Cheddar Gorge and Ebbor Gorge, before finally descending down through the scenic village of Wookey Hole and finishing on the green in front of Wells Cathedral.

Now that I had informed the CHSW fundraising team that we would be embarking on another adventure for them, I decided that the 140-mile run in 2010 would have to take place in May. This should allow me enough time to put in adequate training and be as well prepared as I could ever be in taking on my biggest challenge to date. So, with only eight months until May, I decided to take on the Uphill to Wells Relay and run it solo. Instead of running the route from Uphill to Wells, I would run from Wells to Uphill and then back to Wells, covering 60 miles of hard trail with plenty of ascent to add to the endurance.

Knowing that Martin would be starting the race from Uphill over three different stages – with the slower teams at 10am, middle teams at 12 noon and the faster runners at 2pm – I decided to start at Wells at 2am and aim to be on the beach at Uphill for 10am.

It was a beautiful moonlit morning as I left Wells. Looking back I could see the silhouette of the cathedral shining through the night with the moonlight reflecting on its huge towers that spanned high into the star riddled sky.

My backpack was filled with a hot flask of coffee, several tasty cakes, extra clothing, a foil blanket and a small first aid kit, just in case of an emergency. Several people knew that I would be setting off at that time, and despite such early hours I received many good luck wishes which I read whenever I briefly stopped for a snack.

As I ran across the top of Crook Peak I could see the sun gently emerge from behind the hills, casting her first golden rays of light across the open valleys before me.

Suddenly my legs slammed to a halt. It felt as though I had just run into a fallen tree! As I tumbled through the air I just caught sight of a huge badger scampering off into the distance through the beam of my headtorch, before disappearing into safety.

Crashing to the ground, with my metal flask rolling across the ground in front of me, I checked to see if everything was still in good working order. I then slowly picked myself up and put the flask back into my backpack.

Discovering that I was okay, I started to chuckle to myself as I recalled the grunting noises that came from the badger, and thought how lucky I was not to be able to translate those noises back into English!

It was a very warm morning as the sun continued to rise into the cloudless sky above. The beach was almost deserted as I arrived on the golden sands of Uphill at 9:15am. Deciding not to waste any time for the long steep journey back I phoned Martin and Bob to let them know that I had made it there safely before continuing on my adventure.

After eight miles, I arrived back at Kingswood. On passing a small garage on the main road I refilled my flask and goody bag with savoury snacks for the rest of the run.

Several of the Uphill to Wells relay runners started to pass me and gave me a lot of encouragement, which helped me greatly as the tired legs started to falter on the ascents.

The fresh runners made my pace look pathetic as they scrambled up over the steep slopes ahead. Occasionally I would get a slower runner come up alongside me and I would try and improve my pace to match theirs. But my tired legs were having none of it and I could only watch as they disappeared in front of me.

Ordinary stiles now felt like huge obstacles, and slopes like mountains. As my body began to falter, my mind would play tricks on me and try to convince my body that the run was impossible to achieve. I had been here before and continually fought the angel against the demon, on each shoulder, until the angel won.

Running across a particularly rutted field with huge, dried out holes left by cattle, I became aware of several really painful blisters that had appeared on the ends of my toes. Slowing the run down to large strides, I carefully continued my way across the field until I came to a stile.

I was so glad that I managed to clear that horrible field with my feet in the condition that they were in. But all of a sudden I slipped off the bottom footing of the stile and slammed my toes against a rock. I tried my best to run on, pretending that it hadn't happened, but the pain soon took over. I could feel raw flesh from the front of my toes rubbing against the inside of my trainers every time I put my right foot to the ground. I knew that I had to stop and dress my toes, but now I had been running for over 12 hours on steep terrain, my body ached and my legs felt so tight with the build up of lactic acid.

Hobbling over to a buckled metal gate that had been propped up and looked in as bad a state as myself, I carefully sat on a rail and removed the trainer along with a soggy sock. It looked as though the ends of my toes had exploded, leaving the nails in an extremely uncomfortable situation, and far too painful to even touch. Wrapping a couple of plasters around the wounds and placing a clean dry sock over my foot, I was ready to set off again.

Suddenly the gate gave way, crashing me to the floor. On

impact I let go of my trainer which then spun into the air before disappearing into a patch of stinging nettles! My language became foul as I hobbled around on one leg trying to retrieve my trainer with a broken twig.

With my trainer back in position, I tried to continue, but the pain was excruciating, and my mindset refused to co-operate. Snapping a small branch from the hedgerow, I bit down hard on it and continued with a very clumsy form of jogging. With each step came a reminder that I had only 15 miles still to go.

After what must have been a few miles, I finally spat the stick out, as the nerve endings in my toes had now gone numb and ceased to give me any further significant pain.

Many more runners passed as I got closer to Wells. They, along with the checkpoint marshals, were amazing with all their encouragement for me. Finally, I reached the last section, which was a downhill finish into Wells. This was the section I had been looking forward to for so long. With the pace now quickening, I managed a reasonable looking finish on the Cathedral Green.

After indulging in several cups of tea and endless slices of cake I was presented with a certificate from Martin, for completing the run both ways solo, then hobbled back to find my car.

When I arrived home the first priority was to soak my poor feet in a bowl of really hot salt water, which at first was painful, but proved really satisfying. I was woken up about two hours later with my feet shrivelled up in the cold water, by Richard, a neighbour who had kindly looked after my dogs for the day.

After each long run I would usually get about two weeks respite from the dreaded seizures. Instead of having to get up as many as four times in a single night, I might be lucky and have to get up only once, which felt like an absolute relief.

After further meetings with the CHSW fundraising team we decided the launch of the 140-mile run would be at the end of December. By doing it over the festive period, I knew that I would have a week's holiday from work, and could incorporate another long training run to raise awareness while still having a few days to recover.

For the following two weekends I spent my whole time travelling the 140-mile route to familiarise myself with all the country lanes, and make sure that the route corresponded with the timetable that I would have to follow.

I wanted to start the run from Plymouth Hoe then finish at Radstock, only a mile from where I live.

Carefully I drove the route, noting down the mileage in between various landmarks. Occasionally I would have to park the car and run with Paddo for anything up to eight miles along cycle tracks, like the beautiful route from Bickleigh Bridge in Plymouth up to Yelverton. This runs along an old railway line that features two massive viaducts, offering views across the scenic valleys below.

Another amazing path that I had to run was from Churchinford to Staple Fitzpaine. The path leads down from the main road at the top of the Blackdown Hills for five miles, through some amazing woodland, until it reaches the main road on the boundary of Staple Fitzpaine.

Overnight, Paddo and I would sleep in the car for a few hours after finding a local take-away. He usually ended up with his favourite meal of sausage and chips, then be found snoring away on the top of my sleeping bag.

The next morning, after a fresh brew of tea from the gas stove, we would be on our way again, busily studying map after map, with Paddo sat in the middle of them all on the passenger seat.

What I always found amazing was the amount of time needed to work out and drive the routes. Sometimes plans had to be altered. This would only become apparent after driving or running it.

After two enjoyable weekends away, I was finally happy and content with all the changes. One major issue I discovered with the route turned out to be the total mileage, which had proved to be short.

So now, instead of starting my run from Plymouth Hoe, I would set off from the other side of the Tamar Bridge in the village of Saltash. After several more weeks of planning, I managed to finalise a time schedule to match the 140-mile route.

What I needed to do next was to plan a long training run for December, as this would be my next opportunity for a run of this magnitude while on holiday during the Christmas period.

With all the support that Bob Pearce, the landlord of the Prince of Waterloo pub in Winford, had given me on my 110-mile run, donating free hot drinks and snacks to the support crews and a cheque for £500 to the CHSW team, I wanted to finish my training run at his pub to personally thank him.

As I knew all the main roads and lanes leading out of Winford, this saved me valuable time not having to drive this section of the route. By combining sections of both the 110, and 140-mile routes, I already had pre-written time schedules that would lead me to Exeter, where I planned to start.

I decided my route in December would start from a small village just south of Exeter called Ide, then lead me all the way back over the Blackdown and Mendip Hills, to finish in time for a large dinner some 90 miles later at the Prince of Waterloo pub in Winford.

***

It was a bitterly cold winter's morning as Kevin, a good friend and running companion, drove me to Exeter for the start of my 90-mile training run.

There had been a lot of snowfall overnight, which by now had mostly melted, leaving large puddles of ice cold water along the roadside.

After slowly making our way through the Christmas traffic in Exeter, we arrived in the little village of Ide and proceeded up the narrow high street to the Poachers Inn, where we would start.

While making our final preparations, packing food, drink, extra warm clothing and making sure all our torches and night gear were ready, we were suddenly approached by the BBC news film crew. They had heard about our challenge and decided to come down to film us leaving.

The sky was dark and heavy with storm clouds all around, as the coldest of winds swept through the deserted car park. Every now and then I would shake as a cold chill surged through my body from head to foot.

After a quick filming session for the evening news team, we were on our way at 2.20pm on Tuesday 29th December. We were 20 minutes late departing due to the unexpected filming, but it was a great feeling to know that our efforts would be broadcast all over the South West and raise a lot of awareness for the CHSW team.

Just after leaving the tiny village it began to snow, which quickly turned to sleet, then rain, which felt bitterly cold as it drove in flurries against the exposed skin of our faces. As darkness fell all I could see through the light of my headtorch was sweeping torrents of rain before me.

Village signs became almost impossible to read, until you were virtually touching them, with the rain falling so heavy. About every 10 miles I would seek shelter, anything from a small bus stop canopy to a smoking shelter at the back of a pub, in order to quickly warm up with a cup of coffee and a snack.

I felt so grateful to all the support drivers and runners who later came out to join me through the long, cold and extremely wet night.

As I ran up through the tiny lanes approaching the top of the Blackdown Hills, water came gushing down the steep embankments either side. With the lanes being narrow this resulted in them flooding well over the height of my trainers, giving me very cold and wet feet early into the run.

At midnight the rain was still falling in torrential downpours as we made our way across the Somerset Levels. Sudden gusts of wind would drive the rain straight at you, and I could feel the icy cold water as it trickled down the inside of my jacket.

The most important thing at this stage was to keep going and spend as little time as possible on breaks, otherwise the freezing cold wind would soon chill you to the core, especially as we were all soaking wet through.

In a strange way the wet shirts under my jacket seemed to keep me warm. As long as I kept moving, I seemed to produced enough body heat to maintain a steady temperature.

The brutal steep lanes leading off the Somerset Levels, through the small village of High Ham, were a welcome sight. Although the incline was really tough and required a lot of extra strength, it meant that it would warm me up and help dry out my clothing.

Daylight gradually broke through the dark heavy skies as we approached Wells and the welcoming home ground of the Mendip Hills, but the rain still persisted with its angry torment.

It wasn't until we reached East Harptree, after the long descent down from the Mendips that the rain slowly began to subside, leaving a dark misty atmosphere hanging in the air. But our spirits were far from dark and gloomy, as we had only ten more miles to cover before completing the run, through some of the hardest conditions I had encountered.

Quickly stopping for some final snacks in Chew Stoke, I was so glad to have another fresh cup of tea along with some homemade biscuits that Pat and Chris had made earlier, before coming out to support me to the finish line. The fresh tea tasted so good as I warmed my cold hands around the mug. With each breath taken I could see small clouds forming in the freezing cold air.

The pace quickened as we raced over the final three miles that led down into the village of Winford. Linking hands, we all ran the final 200 metres together, with Bob running alongside us, proudly carrying a huge flag featuring the CHSW logo.

Unknown to us the BBC news crew was waiting at the entrance of the Prince of Waterloo pub, along with landlord Bob Pearce, to welcome us home.

After 22 hours of running across two counties – having remained dry for only two and a half hours throughout the entire run – it felt great to finally finish.

The support teams had done an amazing job again, keeping everyone in high spirits and maintaining a positive outlook through a really bitter winter night.

Our reward, after quickly changing into some dry clothes, was a steak and chips lunch accompanied by a refreshing pint of Guinness in front of a huge log fire.

Later in the week, to my surprise, while fuelling up my car in a local garage, one of the staff members came running across the forecourt with a local newspaper to meet me. "John, have you seen this?" Looking at the front page of the paper, I saw that I had been voted by the local community as the winner of their 'Person of the Year' award.

This was the first award that I had ever won in my entire life and the last thing that I ever expected to hear. I had always thought to myself, throughout all my events, how lucky I was to be able to do them after struggling to walk again.

Constantly I would remember my promise, that if I could, I would always try to help the people I had met during my time at the hospital, who were less fortunate than me.

2009 had proved to be an incredible year in which I had been so fortunate to achieve such amazing results, all made possible by the fantastic team support and encouragement I had behind me.

Crossing the finish line at my first event.

Phil and Steve at the finish of the Midsomer Norton half marathon.

Can't let them beat you! Reading 10K.

Covering the miles while on my first marathon in Snowdonia.

Relaxing Snowdonia views as evening falls.

Training hard in deep snow on the Mendip Hills.

Striding out after running up the stairway to Heaven.

Kayaking at the top of Glastonbury Tor.

Reaching Burnham-on-Sea via kayak as opposed to running.

Ready to start 110 mile run with Jo Pavey.

Support runners join part of the 110-mile run from Barnstaple to Bristol.

Support running at its best with Little Jess.

Yeovilton Air crew delivering a cheque for CHSW.

140-mile run comes to a finish at Radstock.

Steep inclines over Dartmoor.

Completion of the 300-mile run from Land's End to Bath Abbey.

Lonely and dank with a lot of miles still to cover on a 90-mile training run.

Feeling the strain.

Feeling the pain – trying to release the lactic acid from my legs.

Winter four-day run passing Wells Cathedral.

Christmas holiday training run covering 370 miles.

Reunited with Paddo after several days on the road.

Starting off on day one of the world record run.

Bob inspiring me to keep going through the torrential rain.

Airing tired and soaking wet feet while the sun briefly broke through the storm clouds.

Running through country lanes with Paddo.

Only one more day to go after running for five days.

Quick cup of coffee after a 10-minute power nap.

Last 100 metres to cover after running 425 miles.

Celebrating at the doors of Bath Abbey at the end of world record run.

Carrying the Olympic Torch through Frome High Street.

SELF SATISFACTION

With my goal of running 140 miles non-stop in May now launched, I had to make sure that I gave myself enough training to complete the event properly. I didn't want to reach the finish line looking as terrible as I did on my 110-mile run. I wanted to look strong and confident and encourage others into the sport.

Because of the impact inflicted on my body from running continuously on hard roads and country lanes, I wanted to concentrate instead on trail running, which had far less impact on my knees, hips, and back.

Apart from my weekly training sessions with the WCH and MH4 running clubs, I wanted to include three more ultra-runs leading up to May.

The first I decided would be the local Green Man Ultra, which follows the route of the community forest path around Bristol. This scenic route is advertised as 45 miles long by the Forest of Avon Team, who created and maintain the path, although GPS measurements vary from 44-48 miles.

All those who ran the whole 45 miles as individuals or in pairs in under 12 hours earned the title of being called a Woodwose, a Woodwose deriving from an Old English term meaning 'wildman' or 'man of the woods' (regardless of gender).

The second ultra-challenge would be the Wessex Ridgeway which stretches for 68 miles from Tollard Royal to Uplyme.

The third challenge would be combining the West Mendip Way along with the East Mendip Way, a 50-mile run with lots of steep ascents, that starts at the Beach in Uphill and finishes on the bridge over the river Frome, at the bottom of Frome High Street.

The following is my summary of the Green Man Ultra as written in my diary:

***

The day had finally arrived for me to run the Green Man Challenge. Over several previous weekends I ran all eight sections, sometimes joining up two at the same time. A lot of them I ran both ways to become familiar with the route and make it easier to concentrate on my running.

Sunday 14th March 2010

It was a very cold white frosty morning but the sun had started to rise and produce what was to be a perfect day: sunny and clear, with a nice cool breeze to keep the temperature down.

After meeting Chris (The Gaveller) at the start – who would kindly witness my time for the event in order for me to receive my Woodrose certificate if completed under 12 hours – I was on my way.

I started next to the Green Man monument at the top of Ashton Court Estate along with Richard – my first support runner.

Wearing only shorts and a short-sleeved top, I knew I would quickly warm up, especially as I was carrying several bottles of drink, cakes, chocolate bars and spare clothing in case the weather changed for the worst. If I needed anything else, I could phone the support runners who were coming out to join me.

I carried my own gear through five sections as part of my training for the long run in May.

The ascent from the bottom of Long Ashton to the top of Dundry Hill was very demanding on already tired legs, but with no navigational difficulties across the many fields and with clear route markings, we were soon at the top with fantastic views in every direction.

Joining Kevin, my second support runner at Dundry car park, we started to run the next section and were soon on the long descent towards Pensford. The fields were a lot drier than when I had previously run them, and the views were stunning as we looked down through the sun kissed valleys that eventually led to the old railway viaduct in the heart of the village.

Tracey, my third support runner, joined me at the Old Lock Up. Following the tranquil crystal-clear waters of the River Chew, we ran over the old picturesque bridge next to Publow church before passing Compton Dando and on into Keynsham.

Along the route, I kept my energy levels maintained by having regular glucose drinks along with several snacks.

Leaving Tracey at the Lock Keeper Inn in Keynsham, I was joined by Pat and Chris for the fourth section. I felt comfortable and slightly ahead of my planned schedule. The route so far had gone really well without any navigational errors and the fine weather was a real boost to morale, as was the fresh brew of tea that Chris had made for me.

A lot of the fields next to the River Chew were still flooded where the river had broken its banks due to the recent heavy rainfall we had been having, and in some places the trail disappeared and had to be diverted further up into the fields.

I really enjoyed passing the old derelict brickwork buildings and mine shafts around Shortwood Hill. I tried to imagine what they must have looked like when they were operational, especially with the old steam railway that passed through there. Now nature had reclaimed most of it and hidden it from view within her foliage.

The Frome Walkway with Winterbourne Viaduct in the background was a really scenic distraction as we made our way to the White Horse pub in Hambrook. Trying my best to ignore all the fabulous smells coming from the pub as they dished out their roast dinners, I made do with some chocolate bars and another fresh brew from Chris, who had arrived to pick up Pat.

I headed into leg six with Jane, through the more urban areas of Stoke Gifford and Bradley Stoke. Having run these sections in the previous weeks it proved a great help for navigating us through the many pavements and side streets.

With only two more sections to go, I felt a lot more confident and was joined by Bob and Ian who would support me to the finish line.

Having walked half of the long climb up to the top of Clifton Downs previously, I was determined not to let it beat me again. With gritted teeth and a lot of cursing under my breath, I ran the never-ending path to the top. Once on the Downs, my relieved legs sped up a little as we passed the observatory and crossed over the Clifton Suspension Bridge. The views over the Avon Gorge were stunning, and looking around me I could make out several of the landmarks on distant hills I had ran past earlier. Resisting the urge to cheat, we followed the trail around Leigh Woods and joined a mountain bike track back in to Ashton Court Estate to be reunited with the Green Man monument after a surprise sprint finish.

Looking out over Ashton Court and Dundry Hill in the distance, I remembered how we had set off 10 hours and four minutes earlier and according to my watch had now covered 45.42 miles.

A week after submitting a report to the Gaveller, I had my name entered into the honourable order of Woodwoses book as Woodwose XVII and received a stunning certificate for my achievement.

Saturday April 3rd 2010

With a strong wind blowing torrential rain against my bedroom window I had woken up several times during the night. I couldn't help but wonder what state I would find the West and East Mendip Way come daybreak.

Later that morning I was picked up by Ian and John. Both had driven their cars with the intention of leaving John's car at Priddy, with Ian then driving us to Uphill Beach.

We arrived in Uphill for a 6:30am start on a bitterly cold and dark morning. The wind travelling inland off the sea brought with it an instant biting chill to any exposed skin, so we soon got fully dressed with hats and gloves.

Wasting no time, due to the cold temperatures, we set off. The plan for today was to complete the 30-mile West Mendip Way to Wells then continue for another 20 miles along the East Mendip Way, and finish in Frome.

At 8am, after seven miles of running, the skies were still really dark. The trails were covered in huge muddy puddles from all the rain that had fallen in the previous few days. Then it started to rain once again, slowly at first, followed by a continuous heavy downpour, which made conditions under foot even more treacherous.

At 8:30am, wrapped in waterproof jackets and leggings, we were joined by Laurie and Aidan who had braved the atrocious weather to join us for a 15-mile section of the route to Priddy.

Despite the awful weather and conditions, everyone remained in very high spirits, laughing and joking, as each one of us in turn would suddenly lose all traction on the slopes and slide away from the group uncontrollably.

The steep slopes of both Cheddar Gorge and Draycott Hill soon made us forget about the cold wet conditions, as each one of us focused on completing the ascent as best we could.

The rain continued to fall persistently as we entered the quiet village of Priddy. Apart from Jane, Tracey and Kevin, who were waiting patiently for our arrival, the whole place was totally devoid of any sign of life.

Stopping for a 15-minute break I had time to replenish with a few cups of hot coffee, that smelt so good when poured from the flask, carrying its rich fragrance through the damp air.

Heading out with a party of new runners, I thanked Ian and John for all their support, especially for starting off so early in the day with me.

Ebbor Gorge was now very treacherous and the steep steps along with very slippery rocks proved extremely testing on my tired legs.

I felt so glad to arrive in Wells, because I knew the hardest and steepest of the two trails had now been completed. The East Mendip trail would be a lot more forgiving in terms of ascent.

From Wells the route to Shepton Mallet and Cranmore Tower had a lot of flooding, both on the lanes and across several low-lying fields. Several times we were hit, either in the face or all over the front, by a screen of filthy black muddy water, as either myself or one of the others would accidently step into a puddle.

It was now 4:00pm. As we rounded the top corner of the high street, leading out from the village of Chelynch, we had all been hoping the local pub would still be open, but to our dismay it was now shut. Standing patiently in the car park was Bob. Quickly we tried to shelter under the sanctuary of his umbrella, as we watched the weather in disbelief. Torrents of water fell to the ground from the umbrella that would, on occasions, lift with a freak gust of wind.

Jane and Tracey made a quick dash to their car which they had parked there on their way to Wells, while Bob and I just looked at each other silently, questioning whether we should abandon the run.

My uncertain expression soon turned into a grin, and was quickly met by the same reaction from Bob. "Come on then, let's get it over with", he said, as he shook his umbrella and returned it to his car before joining me for the remaining eight miles.

Ploughed fields turned into swamps, with huge lumps of tacky mud that formed layer upon layer on our trainers, adding extra weight that felt like lead. Running across normal fields felt like a luxury as the wet grass quickly removed all the excess debris from our shoes.

As we passed Cranmore Tower, we couldn't even see the top of it through all the low-lying cloud above us.

In some places where we would usually run alongside a gentle stream, we were now running alongside a river with torrents of water flooding over its embankments.

Finally, with no let-up from the awful weather conditions, we reached the outskirts of Frome, where the pavements and side streets proved so much easier to finish our run.

The 50-mile West and East Mendip Way was a run that I had wanted to do for a long time, and finishing it gave me a great feeling of satisfaction despite the bad weather conditions.

Our reward for the 12-hour run was to celebrate in a local café with several hot coffees to warm ourselves up with, then quickly change into dry clothes having been soaked through to the skin most of the day.

Wessex Ridgeway, Saturday 24th April 2010

Four weeks later and with only three weeks to go until my 140-mile run, I did my last big training event which involved running the entire length of the Wessex Ridgeway. It's an event open to running clubs from all over the South West to complete the 68-mile route as a six-stage relay.

Starting at 5am, with a magnificent sunrise, I was joined on the Wessex Ridgeway by members of several running clubs, including WCH, MH4 and Gillingham Trotters. The start was from Tollard Royal near Sherborne in Dorset, and travelled along roads, tracks and fields, with so many stunning views.

The countryside varied dramatically with valleys, hills and historical features such as iron age hill forts and sleepy hamlets.

The run was split into 12 legs of between five and nine miles, with runners volunteering to do two to five legs each.

One of my support runners chose to run eight sections with me and covered a total of 42 sun-baked miles. Various other teams provided the all-important logistical support by ferrying hot and tired runners back and forth from the remotest of locations, while providing much needed snacks and drinks.

My expected finish time was scheduled for 10pm in Uplyme, near Lyme Regis, which allowed 17 hours for the run. But after feeling really strong throughout the event, and finishing with a very quick pace for the final one-and-a-half miles, we managed to come in one hour and 45 minutes early.

I felt completely overjoyed with this achievement, having struggled over many a Dorset hillside. It had been an amazing team effort and I couldn't thank the support crews enough for all their help. My legs felt so tired, especially from all the hills and valleys, with such hot conditions, but inside I felt fantastic, which gave me a real confidence boost for my big run in May.

***

Six years had now passed since I learnt to walk my first mile after recovering from a traumatic bout of seizures. I couldn't believe how fast those years had passed, and all the new adventures that I had been so fortunate to be able to take part in since learning to run.

I was still averaging 60 hours a week in my job as a civil engineer. The rest of my time was taken up either training or organising events. I found most nights I could snatch between five and six hours of sleep especially with all the longer runs that mercifully kept the seizures at bay. To have a good night's sleep felt so refreshing and a sheer luxury that I would never take for granted again.

About six months after my radiotherapy treatment, I also lost, for a few months, my ability to taste food and smell anything. Until then I took these two major senses for granted, but now I had lost them it brought a whole new perspective to life. All food now had no taste whatsoever and was devoid of any flavour.

I tried cooking my favourite meals, hoping that my sense of taste would return, only to end up disappointed time after time as I was left with a permanent metallic-peppery sensation in my mouth. I would curse myself for not appreciating what I had before.

I missed my sense of smell as all the new Spring blossom appeared in the garden. Early in the season I always looked forward to seeing my special collection of my late mother's cottage roses come into bloom. They were so old and never failed to fill my garden with their vibrant fragrance.

Then one day, just as I was beginning to believe that this would be permanent, I began to regain a small amount of taste. At first, I thought it was my imagination playing tricks with me, but slowly and surely my ability to taste food returned, along with my sense of smell.

Every day I would walk the length of my garden to capture the fragrance once more from the roses. Food now meant so much more to me than just a form of fuel. I now felt the happiest person alive and swore that I would never ever take these senses for granted again.

Now with only two weeks left until the start of my 140-mile run, I wanted to raise as much awareness as possible. So on a wet, cold and blustery Friday morning I drove down to Plymouth Hoe with Bob to meet the local community CHSW fundraising team.

While there, we had several interviews with the local press and radio stations to promote the building of 'Little Harbour', a new children's hospice in St Austell. As I took one final glance at the tall red and white lighthouse standing proudly on the Hoe, I couldn't help but wonder how many ships she had seen leaving Plymouth harbour over the years.

A lot of my journey home followed the route that I would use for my run back to Radstock, only next time, I hoped the weather would be kinder, without all the wind and rain.

On several occasions, with the weeks passing by so quickly, I found myself starting to question my ability to run the 140-mile route and doubted achieving my goal.

What I needed was a distraction from all the running, a publicity stunt to promote the event and attract the media's attention by doing something no one else had done before.

My favourite hobby before I was taken ill was to kayak on the South coast, where I also did a lot of free-lung diving along the way. But what unusual kayaking stunt could I do?

It was while I was in Glastonbury, finalising my route through the town, that I noticed a lot of local rivers on the map and came up with the idea of taking a kayak to the top of Glastonbury Tor, before continuing for a trip down one of the local rivers.

I went to see Martin, who kindly promoted my events on his website, and explained to him my mad new idea. A while later he came back with a brilliant route we could all kayak, taking us from Glastonbury all the way to Burnham-on-Sea, following the River Brue.

It was at the start of a really beautiful day, on Saturday 8th May 2010, that I arrived with Martin at the base of Glastonbury Tor as the sun was just beginning to rise into the clear sky.

We decided to take a lighter inflatable kayak to the top of the Tor for our photographs, and were both glad of the choice we made by the time we reached the top.

Covered in sweat, puffing and panting, I managed to position the kayak vertically, right next to the Tor, for Martin to take a photo, when an elderly man approached with his collie dog. With a very confused expression on his face, he lost no time in asking what we were up to and said, "Never in all my years have I ever seen a boat on the top of the Tor before".

With the kayak propped upright in one hand and a large paddle in the other, I replied with a serious expression across my face, "Haven't you seen the weather forecast? They've given a warning about torrential rain coming in."

He released his gaze from me and promptly looked up at the cloudless blue sky above before regaining his focus on me. By now I could no longer hold the serious expression which had rapidly begun to turn into a cheeky smile, to which he replied, "You stupid buggers. I thought you were being serious for a moment", before ambling away.

On looking down, I was just in time to see his collie dog slowly lowering his back leg from the kayak, where he left a large yellow puddle soaking into the ground.

Shrugging my shoulders, I looked back across at Martin, who continued with a smile to take more photographs.

Apart from the fellow with his dog, there was only one other person up that early on top of the Tor, a young lady oblivious to us, who performed what looked like very relaxed yoga movements while standing on one leg!

After a quick descent from the Tor, we made our way over to the nearby River Brue, where we met up with six other people who had arrived with their kayaks to complete the journey to Burnham-on–Sea with us.

It was so peaceful as we travelled along the river. Looking back over my shoulder I could see the Tor slowly disappearing in the background. The tranquil surface of the crystal clear water reflected the sun as lush green embankments weaved through the silent countryside.

In some places the river was really shallow and we could easily see the bottom, while at others it was deep and surrounded by overhanging trees that dipped their branches into the silent water.

On several occasions I caught sight of the distinctive turquoise colours of a kingfisher, as it quickly glided away from us.

By the end, the cruise had taken us from Glastonbury to Meare, East Huntspill, Highbridge and finally onto Burnham-on-Sea where we looked out across the Bristol Channel.

***

Time passed very quickly over the following five days, with a mixture of work, assembling the last of my kit and several media interviews to attend to.

After finishing work on Thursday night and checking that everything was in place for the following day, I went out with some friends for a large meal in one of my favourite pubs, to prepare for the long journey ahead of me.

Driving home from the Mendip Hills after indulging in a 22oz steak, it seemed almost impossible that, after 10 months of organising, I was about to embark on the biggest run of my life – 140 miles non-stop. There were only seven hours remaining!

Friday 14th May, 2010

At 1:45am, I was on my way to Cornwall, kindly driven by Kevin and accompanied by Bob, who would remain with me throughout the entire run. On the journey down I had plenty of time to reflect on what was ahead of me, while I tried to catch snippets of sleep.

Standing at the entrance to Victoria Gardens in Saltash, it was fast approaching my start time of 5am. I remember looking out into the darkness, then over to the Tamar Bridge with its bright lights highlighting the huge structure before me. For the first time I suddenly felt really nervous about what the next 38 hours would entail.

Clutching a laminated timetable, that neatly rolled up in the palm of my hand, I could immediately check my running pace at any time during the run.

The time arrived and I started my journey off down through the brightly lit High Street of Saltash. As the Tamar Bridge saw me out of Cornwall with the dawn breaking all around us, I felt so small compared to this huge feat of engineering that towered above me. Picturing the big pile of maps that I had used to work out my route, I had a similar feeling about this run, of how small I was, compared to the huge expanse of terrain ahead of me.

The drizzle didn't dampen our spirits or lessen the beauty that Plymouth sea front had to offer us that morning. Following the West Devon Way footpath, with the River Plym in the background, we ran over to Marsh Mills and then onto the steady climb through Bickleigh Vale and on into Clearbrook. Here we had to depart from local support runner Jo Jenkins, who had kindly guided me and Bob all the way up from Plymouth Hoe.

Yelverton soon approached, where we met up with two mobile crews who would support me all the way back to Radstock.

A steep climb followed, up the unforgiving road that leads through Sharpitor, then I had the full attention of Dartmoor ahead of me and knew it wasn't going to give me an easy time.

Waves of rain now swept across the hillside on gusts of bitterly cold wind. Despite this, I felt this showed the true rugged beauty of Dartmoor. With dark rolling clouds threatening above, it was a stark reminder that mother nature was in charge.

Glancing back, I could just make out the coastline of Plymouth through the misty haze, before our arrival in Princetown. The first marathon distance had now been completed with another four-and-a-half to go.

On our journey through Postbridge, I couldn't resist the temptation to cross the old Medieval clapper bridge that spans the East Dart River, as I wondered how many people must have crossed this magnificent stone structure before us.

Approaching the isolated and remote Warren House Inn, which stands at 1425ft above sea level and is the highest Inn in Southern England, I stood for a brief while to admire the scenic views in all directions. Looking ahead of me, I couldn't help but notice how the road ahead disappeared and then reappeared, as many as three times, indicating the sheer rise and fall of the local terrain.

Dropping down off the moors, the weather was starting to change with the rain slowly giving way to clearer skies. My reward for reaching the Pony Centre, on the way to Moretonhampstead, where we were due the next break, was a pony biscuit, given to me mistakenly and devoured along with several other snacks during the rush to get going again! Apparently one of the girls only realised when she went back to feed her favourite pony as we were leaving!

As we ran through the town of Moretonhampstead I felt we were comfortably well on our way into the run, after already having covered 40 miles. But just five miles further down the road on the approach to Meadhay, I noticed that I had suddenly become very tired and every part of me began to struggle with the pace.

I tried to hide this from everyone around me and kept running with a smile, but inside I was struggling. This was a shock to me as I hadn't felt like this on any of my training runs. Several things suddenly sprung to mind. Had I overdone all the training runs leading up to this without leaving enough recovery time? Had I got the nutrition wrong? Had I gone too long without any sleep? This was now 12 hours into the run and I hadn't slept properly for a day-and-a-half.

I quickly came to the conclusion that I had become complacent during the run, and hadn't focused properly on what I was doing, with all the distraction that was going on around me.

The remedy for this was ahead of me, a huge valley to climb, with several steep hills. It was going to be the valley or me that would come out the winner. I hadn't done ten months of hard training to be defeated by some foreign hill!

An hour later we started the steep climb. With support runners chasing me to keep up the gruelling pace, we managed to overcome the hills, the tiredness, and all the aches and pains. I had literally run through the biggest psychological barrier of the whole event.

Running through Exeter, we passed the second marathon distance landmark and felt confident we were well on schedule. With all the support from the runners alongside me and the small groups of people who came out in the towns and villages, the atmosphere was simply amazing.

Arriving in Broadclyst, I prepared for the evening ahead, donning headtorch, lights, and reflective jacket and bottoms. As darkness fell, it felt like a lifetime ago that I watched the dawn break as we crossed the Tamar Bridge.

Deep in thought, I suddenly realised that a car had pulled up alongside me. As the window slowly wound down, a hand appeared clutching a large bag of chips. It was Paul, the Chairman from Wells running club, who had come to support me. Clutching the warm bag of chips tightly in one hand while eating with the other, I slowly ran up the steep hill ahead of me, while sharing my supper with two other support runners.

The chips proved to be an excellent form of fuel and kept me going through the long cold night ahead.

From Cullompton we then passed through Uffcombe before starting the steep climb to the top of the Blackdown Hills. At 1:30am on Saturday morning I was greeted unexpectedly with a cool glass of Guinness from a very kind group of people in the village of Churchinford and celebrated in true style having passed the third marathon landmark.

Running along the quiet country lanes at 3am with my support runners, I couldn't help but wonder about the local wildlife, especially as we headed down through a large forest trail at Staple Hill. It was at this stage that I passed the rumour back through the support runners that bears always like to feed on the person at the very back of the group!

A very tight group of runners later emerged out onto the main road from the dense forest on the outskirts of Staple Fitzpaine. The village was sound asleep when we passed through, as the night slowly gave way to a brand new day. This was the first time I had run non-stop while having seen the sun rise, set, then rise again.

The dawn brought a spectacular sunrise, which highlighted some amazing sights, such as the mist rising up from the Somerset Levels and the ruins of an old church that stood proudly on the top of a steep hill, known as Burrow Mump.

After climbing a short hill leading to the village of Othery, we stopped and I handed Rita, one of my support runners, a birthday card from my backpack. Then as a double celebration, I opened a bottle of champagne to celebrate her birthday as well as crossing the 100-mile landmark of our run.

Five minutes later the leading support crews returned only to find us having a party at 7:45 in the morning.

That wasn't the only surprise that Othery had for us that morning. As we passed through the village, I was greeted by a group of supporters and presented very kindly with a huge jar of pickled onions by one of them. I decided to save them until after the run and handed them over to the support crew. I couldn't be that cruel to my support runners!

Reaching High Ham was a great relief, as the village certainly lives up to its name. We had now passed the fourth marathon landmark.

Having passed along the two-and-a-half-mile mile straight of Butleigh Moor, we then climbed another steep hill leading to Ivythorne. I had now run 110 miles – further than I had ever run before – and I felt so much better than when I had finished my 110-mile run a year ago.

Everything felt really good at this point. I had to be very careful to make sure I did the vital stretching at various intervals, to help keep the body supple and prevent seizures.

As I arrived in Glastonbury, I felt that all the hard training over the previous ten months had really paid off. It was a very sunny Saturday morning and I was given a great welcome from the crowds and my new team of support runners. I met Richard and his partner Vicky who were joining me to run their first marathon back to Radstock. It seemed the perfect day, especially as they had brought along my little dog Paddo, who I hadn't seen for some 32 hours.

Running up through Wells High Street was just one of the many highlights that I remember. Now on home ground, the Cathedral looked magnificent as we stood before her with her towers reaching up into the blue sky.

Replenishing myself with several more snacks to maintain my energy levels, we made our way up the Old Bristol Road, with its unforgiving steep climb, to the top of the Mendip Hills.

Having reached 125 miles within 33 hours, this was now the last major hill that I would have to encounter.

Passing by the huge Penn Hill television mast always brings me a happy feeling, as many a time she has welcomed me home with her array of lights, visible for miles through the darkness.

After a welcome break at the Hunter's Lodge in Priddy, and a pint of refreshing ale from Roger and Jackie, I was soon on my way, passing the sparkling Priddy ponds, whose cool waters looked so inviting.

Running steadily over Smitham's Hill, which leads down off the Mendips to East Harptree, I had Jessica, my cousin's little daughter, holding tightly onto my hand. She guided me through each painful step as we descended the steep unforgiving slopes that seemed to pull on every fibre of my body.

A really warm reception greeted us as we passed through the gentle streets of East Harptree. Old friends and new faces greeted us on our long journey, which filled me with a sense of warmth.

Passing the clock tower and heading down the narrow high street, I suddenly felt another little hand grasp hold of mine. Looking down I saw that it was Katie, Nicola's little daughter, who wanted to run with us since passing through Moretonhampstead. Her big smiles and endless energy were a real inspiration over the next couple of miles and led us pass the fifth marathon landmark.

Approaching Chewton Mendip, I looked out for the church tower, which highlighted the village's skyline, before passing through several narrow country lanes that eventually ended up at Emborough Church and the huge fishing ponds.

At the Old Down Inn, I now had only six miles to go to reach the finish line. Again I felt in really good condition considering the number of hours and punishment I had put my poor body through.

On passing Midsomer Norton Rugby Club, I felt so happy to be near to home, but at the same time my heart felt really heavy as I ran a lap of honour around the rugby pitches for my two cousins, who had both played in rugby fixtures here. I then felt so much happier as I recalled several of Phil's comments from my memory.

As I left the club, I had a great send-off from the crowd of supporters, wishing me well as I tackled the final few miles. On entering the bottom of Midsomer Norton High Street, I could see several CHSW banners being waved frantically in the air by their representatives. Their supporting cheers made me really emotional, and with a strong sense of pride I was truly welcomed home.

The last mile I can only describe as remarkable. I had now run 140 miles non-stop, well over five marathons, and 30 miles further than I had previously run, plus met some of the kindest people in the whole of the South West.

The finish line at the Miners Wheel monument came into sight as we rounded the last corner into Radstock. Just before crossing the final road that led up to the Wheel, I said a massive "thank you" under my breath. There were people everywhere I looked welcoming us home and the atmosphere was incredible.

While having team photographs by the Miners Wheel, I looked around at all the runners, and noticed Richard and Vicky, who had managed to complete their first ever marathon that day.

Also, I noticed that Paddo my dog was firmly snuggled down in my arms and wasn't going to let me out of his sight. All the way back from Glastonbury he had been in the lead support vehicle passenger seat, with his head out of the window, looking back at me as if to say "keep going old man".

In the 10 months leading up to this event, I had covered 3,500 miles of training, which was worth every step. As well as raising a huge amount of awareness for the CHSW charity, it had brought in thousands of pounds once again to support their vital funding.

I had now found a whole new passion for ultra-running. It showed me how much I was capable of pushing myself to extreme limits. Having had such amazing support to back me along the journey I was now inspired even more.

NO TRAINING LIKE REAL TRAINING

I found that my time was now being taken up not only with training, but also answering an increasing number of emails that I would receive from complete strangers. They would ask me how I first got involved in long distance running and what my secrets were to keep going during hard times.

With so many emails and enquiries from people that I had met while out on my long runs I came up with the idea of giving a public talk one evening.

At first, I dismissed the idea and reminded myself how much I dreaded giving talks to fellow classmates back at school. Being a shy and reserved kind of person, I didn't like being the centre of attention, especially in a room full of people. I could just about get away with it while out on my events, by being one amongst a large number of runners all in a pack.

Without mentioning a word of this to anyone, I was approached by the CHSW fundraising team asking if I could give a talk. It would be to a group of runners who were very nervous about completing their first half marathon in Bristol.

I immediately agreed but it was only after leaving the team at Charlton Farm that I began to question myself about what I had just agreed to do. Slowly getting into my car, I told myself that it was too late, I had agreed to do it. With all the smiles of the grateful staff, how could I turn back around and tell them I had changed my mind?

Two weeks later, after giving the hospice time to promote the talk, I found myself sitting before a room full of people and the centre of attention.

At first, I felt really uncomfortable as I made eye contact with everyone in the room. Only minutes before the room had been filled with laughter and conversation, but now there was complete silence.

I noticed my sweaty hands begin to shake, as the pages that contained my talk started to quiver under my tight grasp. The silence remained until I plucked up enough courage to finally introduce myself and explain the reason why I was there that evening.

I immediately knew that if I attempted to read my notes the talk would go horribly wrong, so I decided to tell my story from the heart instead. An hour later I still had the full attention of everyone in the room, raising laughter from the more comical events that had happened to me, and complete silence as I dealt with the more serious aspects of my life.

Realising that it was time to close the talk, I rounded the evening off with a series of questions and answers. After finishing I couldn't believe that I wanted the talk to continue even longer, especially having been so negative at the start.

Over the summer period I decided to keep up my new-found confidence, by giving more talks to groups and visiting local schools to promote sporting activities. I had to cut down on my long distance training due to the lack of time available.

Gradually it became more noticeable that my body was slowing down again, and sure enough the seizures started to return. At first, I dismissed the pains. Perhaps I had lifted something heavy at work and this was now giving me back pains? It could be that I had been overworking and had far less time to relax, especially as I was now giving public talks in any available free time.

Deep down I knew that I had to face my situation head on and accept the fact, whether I liked it or not, that my seizures were returning and I needed to increase my mileage once again.

In September entries were open for the Uphill to Wells relay once more, where teams of six run the 30-mile route. Last year, to increase my training, I ran the route both ways, covering 60 miles. But this time I wanted to increase the mileage even further, and finish at the same time as all the other contestants.

This being the second year the event had been held, I decided I would increase my route from 60 to 80 miles, and promote the run for Martin, who spent so much time organising it.

In order to increase the total mileage to 80, I would have to run 20 miles to Wells then double the circuit by running to Uphill then back to Wells again.

After hours of measuring various maps, I decided my run would start in Bath city centre, next to the Abbey, then continue the 20-mile journey on to Wells Cathedral. From there I would join the West Mendip Way to Uphill before returning back on the same circuit.

Hopefully a run of this magnitude would bring an abrupt end to the annoying seizures and give me back the freedom of a good night's sleep.

Friday 24th September 2010.

As Vicky, my neighbour, kindly dropped me off in the brightly lit centre of Bath at 8:30pm, I couldn't help but notice how much of a hill we had descended into the city.

Hundreds of times I must have driven this route, but now seeing it as a passenger brought a lot more detail to light. Standing before Bath Abbey, magnificently silhouetted against a full moon, I was amazed at how quiet the city was, especially for a Friday evening. I managed to pester a young couple to take a photograph of me with my phone so I could prove that I had started in Bath and not in my hometown of Westfield.

When the couple enquired as to what I was doing, I got as far as telling them that I was running from Bath to Wells when their expressions changed. I left it at that and didn't tell them the rest of the story.

At 9pm I set off down through the streets of Bath and was soon leaving the bright lights as I climbed my way up and out of the city.

Eight hours earlier in the day I had to have some back teeth removed to help cure a bad jaw infection. On the advice sheet it recommended that I didn't drink any alcohol for 24 hours. This I was very good at, as I ran past many pubs and bars. The other recommendation was that I should rest for 24 hours, which I was not so good at following!

Settling into the run helped me forget, and was a great distraction from the aches and pains my jaw was giving me. If things did get too painful, I could always pull out of the run after just ten miles at my home in Westfield.

Two hours later, I was picking up my backpack containing spare clothes, drinks and food for the rest of the journey. Although the day before I had dropped off some supplies en route, the backpack still seemed quite heavy.

Richard, my neighbour, agreed to run with me from Westfield to Wells and was great company after two hours of solo running, beside the fact that I had his favourite chocolate bars on board.

On my backpack I had attached my Union Jack flag, which fluttered above me. So far we had been stopped three times by motorists asking who we were representing, as other cars blew their horns as they passed.

At 1am, I left Richard with his car outside Wells Cathedral and continued the steep climb up through the darkness into Ebbor Gorge. In the beam of my headtorch I could see all the bats come in to feed on the insects around me.

By 3am, I was running through the deserted village of Priddy. The whole area was brightly lit by a huge full moon. There was no need for a torch as everything was so clearly visible under the moon's silvery glow.

It was now 5am as I ran across the top of the famous Cheddar Gorge, constantly slipping on the smooth rock surface as I descended down a steep trail. Leading out from Black Rock, I finally reached the softer surface of a valley known as Velvet Bottom.

Six miles further on I reached a remote area called Kingswood, I now needed my headtorch for the first time in what seemed like ages. Entering into the darkness of a small forest, the tree canopy sheltered me from the moonlight, secretly hiding the huge protruding tree roots that were ready to snag any unsuspecting prey.

As I left the forest, it was like stepping out of a tunnel. On approaching Crook Peak the full moon now lit the countryside for miles around, especially on either side of the huge ridgeway. The only sound that could be heard was the gentle flutter coming from my flag as a cool breeze swept up through the valley below. I stopped for a brief moment to absorb the special moment. It would have been so easy to have just run on and miss the sheer beauty of it all.

As I gazed up at my flag, some two feet above me, I felt a strange sense of pride watching the colours as they caught the moonlight. My attention was then distracted by the endless star-filled sky. Even the grass sparkled with the magic touch of a frost. It was almost as if I had stumbled into another strange magical world since leaving the forest.

As the night sky slowly gave way, the first golden rays of sun started to appear over the horizon, which soon spread out before me, covering the terrain in a blanket of warmth

Descending from the Ridgeway, I now had a steady downhill section that would lead me through the village of Bleadon, then finally onto the golden sands at Weston-super-Mare.

The first thing that caught my eye was a snack van that had just opened on the side of the beach. With visions of a fresh brew of tea immediately springing to mind, I quickly made my way over, only to be thoroughly disappointed, as they only sold cold cans of drink and wouldn't be cooking for at least half an hour. This is England! Whatever happened to the good old cup of tea?

Trying to hide my disappointment, I reached for my partially filled flask and poured a tepid black coffee, while muttering a few words (that cannot be repeated) about snack bar owners only serving cold drinks on a frosty morning!

It was now 9:30am and after texting Martin to let him know I was leaving Uphill for the solo race entry, I was on the return journey back up the long climb to Bleadon. Passing along the narrow wild paths, I was greeted by several horse riders making the most of a perfect sunny morning, before eventually reaching Loxton.

Seventy miles had passed when Draycott presented its relentless hill. By now my legs felt very weak and I knew I had to focus really hard to complete this challenge. Reaching for supplies, I quickly devoured several chocolate bars, along with an energy drink, then with the help of a free supply of fresh blackberries that lined the hedgerows, I managed to conquer this beast of a climb.

Draycott Hill – from the war memorial at the bottom right up to the fields on top leading to Priddy – is one of those hills that, half-way up, make you feel as if your legs want to disown you, especially after a few miles of running!

It felt really good to have the company of other runners, as the first teams caught up with me, even though they made me look as if I was stood still as they went by so fast. Wells was now visible, only a stones throw away, and with the company of other runners we ran through the city to finish in front of the Cathedral.

Finally, after collecting a fresh brew of tea, which had been constantly on my mind since leaving Weston beach that morning, it was now time to reflect on the past 21 hours of solo running.

After experiencing seizures before my last 80-mile run, the following two months had been really good, I now felt really fit and healthy, on a level that I had never experienced before.

I noticed on the last Uphill to Wells relay that more solo runners had taken part than the previous year. The trend seemed to be for more people wanting to run an ultramarathon.

A few times I received emails or phone calls from the media enquiring if I had any big challenges or plans lined up for 2011, and if I did then they would help me with publicity.

This was my dream now becoming a reality, especially when I thought back to my very first nervous phone call to a local newspaper asking if they were interested in covering the story of my very first run, some six years earlier.

The last three ultra-runs that I had organised had raised thousands of pounds and a huge amount of awareness for the remarkable work carried out by CHSW. But now I could also show people that even after a serious illness, you can still achieve incredible goals in life, if you truly believe in yourself.

One of the many great memories that stuck in my mind with the 140-mile run was, how the residents in the small village of Churchinford, on the Blackdown Hills, waited for me to arrive in really atrocious weather conditions. It was in the early hours of the morning and they patiently waited to welcome and encourage the support crews and myself into their village and greet us with food, drinks and even provided warmth to us with a cosy log fire.

As an acknowledgement to the village, I arranged for all the crew and me to meet up again and have a meal in the York Inn, Churchinford, to personally thank them all.

On Friday 20th November, I had a 70-mile training run planned. This time I would start at Bath Abbey and finish in Churchinford, hopefully in time to celebrate with one of their tasty steak meals.

Bath – Churchinford – 70 miles, 20th November, 2010

Walking out from the car park in Bath, approaching the main shopping precinct at 2:15am, the wind was freezing cold, but at least the heavy rain had passed leaving us with just some light drizzle.

Jane, Tracey and myself had just broken into a steady jog up to the Abbey, which was going to be our start location, when suddenly we were greeted by a large group of cheering night club revellers who were on their way home. Their support and encouragement were most welcome with optimistic chants like, "keep going, you can make it", and "not far to go now", when in fact we had only run

50 metres from the car park and hadn't even reached the start of our 70-mile run!

At 2:30am we set off from the large fountain outside the Abbey and made our way through the main shopping precinct, that looked amazing with all the Christmas lights. In high spirits we ran out of the city, as the rain started to come down heavier. At least we were warm and running at a comfortable pace.

A police car illuminated the road around us with its flashing blue lights as it passed, in recognition of our efforts.

Approaching Radstock, I looked up at the flag I was carrying on top of my backpack. It clung to the standard, soaking wet and refusing to reveal its colours in protest at the awful weather.

Richard greeted us at the bottom of Radstock Hill and with a smile said: "I thought you might be ahead of schedule."

Snatching a quick drink from my flask, and thanking the others for coming out so early to give their support, Richard and I departed on our way, leaving the others to retrieve their cars. Approaching the Old Down Inn, about an hour later, we were passed by a car blowing its horn and flashing its lights frantically. It turned out to be the other three support runners finally on their way home.

With the rain now falling hard, we were struggling to see which direction we were going in, with only a desperate scattering of torchlight trying to penetrate the storm before us.

The weather showed no sign of giving in, with little trickles of water now running down my back. My leggings guided water down the inside of my legs and into my already sodden trainers.

Stopping outside the Old Down Inn at 5:30am, I sought sanctuary under a large oak tree to have a quick intake of food and drink. Suddenly a large gust of wind swept through the area and immediately soaked me with freezing cold rain as the tree emptied its sodden branches.

By now, I was starting to get really cold, I could see the steam clouding up from inside our jackets in the torchlight. Should I continue? Or should I abandon the run because of the severe weather conditions?

I decided to continue. We had already covered 14 miles with support crews who had given up their time and I wasn't going to let them down. A lot of planning had gone into organising this event and I hated the thought of letting anybody down, especially when there was a large steak meal waiting for us at the end.

I had a spare set of dry clothes with me, but I didn't want to use them just yet as I didn't know how long this storm was going to last, especially with such a long way still to go.

By increasing my pace up the road to Emborough, I gradually started to warm up and feel comfortable again. Turning a sharp corner by Emborough church, we were greeted by a flood that covered the whole of the lane ahead, which left us with no other option but to run through the freezing water.

At 7am,with 22 miles now completed, the first signs of daylight began to appear. The rain had now eased off but the air hung thick with moisture and a freezing fog.

By 9am I had arrived at Wells Cathedral and had to run solo for the next 22 miles. Before continuing, I found a local bakery. After two cups of tea, two sausage rolls, two beef pies, and two cream doughnuts, I made my way out of the shop and my flag scraped across the ceiling until it found freedom again outside. I am sure the lady who served me thought that I was buying enough supplies to fuel up a whole running team.

Wiping the rain from a bench in St Cuthbert's churchyard, I sat down and tucked into a really good breakfast.

Ten minutes later, and surrounded by a few very disappointed pigeons, I got up to place all the empty wrappers into a nearby litter bin. It was then that I saw several empty beer bottles and cans strewn around the floor by the bench, that I hadn't noticed in my haste to 'dine out'. People walking past must have thought that I had been there all night having my own party, especially while looking totally bedraggled, supporting a large backpack beside me with the flag acting as bunting!

Making a quick exit, I made my way to Glastonbury, where I met Kevin who had kindly brought me a fresh flask of coffee and bacon sandwiches. It was acts of kindness like this that really inspired me and filled me with the determination to achieve my goals.

As I ran through the village of Street a lady shouted out from her window that she had heard my interview on the radio and wanted me to come over. Cautiously I approached her driveway, where she came out to give this soggy individual a donation, and told me how she had waited for me to pass through.

I tried to convince myself that the backpack was getting lighter with every mile, because of all the food resources that were being used up, but it certainly didn't feel like it.

The long straight road that stretches across Butleigh Moor for two miles still played its tricks on me. The harder I focused my attention on the long straight road, the more I was convinced I could see the end. But in reality, it never seemed to surrender, even if I tried to run it at a faster pace. To overcome this I reminded myself that when I did reach the end, I would reward myself with a large cream cake that I had somehow resisted from the top of my backpack. Running several miles with a fresh cake only inches from my head when really hungry wasn't easy.

Feeling really fed up drinking stale coffee from a flask at the top of High Ham, I decided to treat myself to a delicious pint of ale in the local pub. I was ahead of time anyway, and I was hot, and I had a heavy backpack, and…!

Exiting the pub, a bitter chill from a cruel wind soon reminded me that there was no time to waste in order to keep warm.

Othery Church spire stood proudly in the distance as I descended the steep but short hill from High Ham on the southern side, to join the busy main road once again. Soon I was greeted by the welcome sound of car horns, which was a great confidence booster and reassured me that I wasn't on my own.

Just as the really cold and damp evening began to approach, I was joined by several support runners who kept me going at a comfortable pace as we began the ascent over the Blackdown Hills.

Along with the darkness of the evening, a thick blanket of fog began to descend around us. Quickly looking back over the valley below us I could still see the church spire at Staple Fitzpaine lit up as one of my landmarks.

Running as if almost blind through the eerie fog, my headtorch lit up an old wooden signpost partially hidden in the overgrown hedgerow. On closer inspection it showed that Churchinford was now only two-and-a-half miles away. I immediately pictured a large juicy steak sat on a full plate of delicious chips, just waiting for me only a short distance up the road in the comfort of the York Inn.

We ran on for what seemed a while before encountering another rather crooked old sign post showing once again that Churchinford was two-and-a-half miles away. I looked at the other runners, who were staring back at me in disbelief. We knew we were on the right road but according to the signs the mileage wasn't getting any less. Not long after, we passed another sign stating Churchinford was one-and-a-quarter miles away – at last the mileage was finally reducing! But further on again we came across yet another sign stating that we had one-and-a-half miles still to travel! Was the mysterious fog playing tricks with us on this forbidding night?

A despondent group of runners now ran through the fog-filled lanes, closely followed by the support car keeping us safe from any traffic approaching from behind. Suddenly through all the swirling mist, we could just make out the lights of a little village ahead of us. Immediately, without uttering a word, the pace quickened as the group sprinted down into the village, finishing at the doorstep of the York Inn.

After a fantastic welcome from everyone, we changed into dry clothes and sat in front of a blazing log fire with a cool Guinness in hand and fine steaks being cooked in the kitchen.

I had contemplated running back home some five hours earlier, but looking at the road conditions with the fog, plus the fact that I had lost two toe nails, I decided that it wasn't worth the risk.

I was happy that I had managed to cover 70 miles in those conditions, 50 of them carrying 28lbs of kit. Now was the time to sit back, relax and enjoy the meal, there would be plenty more opportunities ahead.

***

With each and every run that I carefully planned, scanning maps for hours on end – often into the early hours of the morning – I found a new sense of excitement.

I loved the challenge of being able to run further than anyone else that I personally knew. If I carried on running my half and full marathons I would never be at the top end of the sport. But with ultramarathon running I could push the boundaries further than I could ever have imagined, keep my health in shape and raise funding for children's charities.

With every run that I completed – it didn't matter what mileage it was – I would always say a personal "thank you" at the end. I considered myself to be so lucky in life and remembered that very first walk up the garden without medication and the pain and determination I went through to achieve that one goal. I had been so fortunate to come so far since those first few steps.

The excitement of each new challenge became almost like a craving that swept over me. I would chase mile after mile and when I finally achieved my new target, I would want an even bigger target than before. Even though I could remember each one individually, thinking that they alone might be impossible to accomplish. The main thing that I wanted to prove was that I was still in control of my body and the situation with my seizures. By doing this I could prove to others in the same situation just what could be achieved.

I had proved to myself that I could run 110 miles back in 2009, then achieved 140 a year later, and now a 70-mile training run I could do with only last-minute preparation.

What if I could run 70 miles a day for three days and exceed 200 miles non-stop? This is when I really started to question myself. Was I now expecting far too much for my body to cope with?

People were already telling me that I was pushing myself far too hard and that I should be satisfied with what I had achieved. Several times during the middle of the night I would wake up and ask myself the same question, and memories of severely blistered feet and damaged muscles would come flooding back. But I still felt the irresistible urge to accomplish the impossible. When others told me that I must be completely mad for taking on such events this made me even more determined and fuelled me with an even greater passion to succeed.

For weeks on end I studied my maps, endlessly working out timetables and schedules, but still didn't tell anyone about my ambitions.

Finally, I came to the conclusion that I wouldn't be happy with myself unless I tried to break the 200-mile barrier in just three days.

I knew that the week after Christmas I would be off from work with holiday, so that would be my next window of opportunity. But at the same time, I didn't want people to think I expected them to join me during their Christmas break, especially with it being such a special time for families. So, to overcome this, I reserached which garages, bakeries, and stores would be open throughout the festive season. I also planned several food drop-off points en route that would make me virtually self-sufficient.

If I used routes that I had previously ran, that would make it far easier in a lot of ways. Mentally I had already conquered them and I knew what lay in store for me.

With only a month now to go, I made the decision to try and

run 80 miles a day for two days, covering either another 80 or 65 miles on the third. The third day's mileage would depend on the all-important weather conditions and my physical circumstances.

Cautiously, I drove over to Bob's house to break the news to him. After explaining every detail and showing him that I had thought through every aspect of the run, I could see his face light up as the expression 'here we go again' began to reappear.

Bob was my foundation for every event that I dreamt up. He was always there for me and as long as he believed in me then I knew it would be possible.

All my handwritten timetables I would pass over to him, which he would then transfer to computer and print off for everyone involved, as well as organising all the essential logistics.

Over the Christmas period I had no restrictions at all as to what I ate. It didn't matter if I did very little exercise and consume vast amounts of food, because on the morning of 27th December, I would start my 200-mile run and need every ounce of strength available to me.

225-mile run, Monday 27th December, 2010

After a restless night's sleep I made sure that I had all my running gear ready for each day that I came back home to shower and change. My neighbours very kindly agreed to look after my dogs and gave me a lift into Bath where I made my way to the Abbey for a 6am start.

Standing outside the Abbey once more, I had to keep moving as the wind chill seemed to cut through all my layers of clothing. The car had registered -7°C on the way in, and the pavements were covered in ice with a light sprinkling of snow making conditions even more treacherous.

At 6am I started my adventure, carefully picking my way through the icy streets, with the sound of snow and ice crunching under each step. As I made my way out of the city, I passed queues of people waiting outside some of the stores, ready for the Christmas sales to open and reveal all the latest bargains.

On the long climb out of Bath, I felt my phone vibrating from inside the warmth of my jacket. A local radio station had heard about my run and asked me for a live interview.

I always enjoyed the interviews and the chance for friendly banter mixed with the seriousness of the message I was trying to convey.

Five hours later and I had covered 27 miles, which had been a great start, despite the freezing temperatures. I felt warm with the correct clothing and safe carrying of 28lbs of kit, which was essential as I would be running solo for most of this event.

The day remained very dark as the sky filled with heavy storm clouds which blocked any trace of sunshine or view. Looking up for the Mendip Hills, all I could see was menacing clouds.

My first break, I decided, would be at my brother's house in East Harptree. I had purposely missed the previous scheduled stop in order to give me extra time here and enjoy my sister-in-law, Heather's, Christmas cake! After several cups of tea and a huge slice of cake, I was away running the height of the Mendips once more.

Halfway up the unforgiving climb, I encountered the low-lying cloud that restricted any visibility and hid the snow-covered roads. This made the running conditions really treacherous, as my shoes just slid on the snow and ice, making every step twice the effort.

Apart from the gentle breeze fluttering through my flag the whole countryside stood in complete silence. The further I ran, the worse the conditions got, until I eventually came across a 'road closed' sign where the snow came up to knee height.

I had to quickly make the decision whether to carry on with the planned run or whether to abandon the whole idea because of the severe weather conditions.

If I cancelled the run, I wouldn't have the chance again of having three spare days off work, unless I lost even more of my holiday time. Perhaps if I carried on down off the Mendips, the roads might gradually get better, like they were on the way out from Bath.

Having come so far into the run, I decided to carry on and make my way down off the other side of the Mendip Hills. I had sufficient spare warm clothes and supplies with me, and I knew several people who lived in towns and villages that I would be passing through if I needed anything else.

Descending the steep lanes, I had several near misses on the ice. Performing pirouettes with a heavy backpack made me keep my wits about me as I finally reached Wells. The roads were now relatively clear of snow and ice, but it was replaced by slushy ice-cold water, which persistently flooded my trainers.

Even though I was running alone through atrocious weather conditions, I was still ahead of my planned schedule, which kept me positive. There had been very little traffic on the deserted roads, but the occasional motorist would recognise me running with the flag and fill me with inspiration by blowing their horn, or slowing down to cheer me on. Whenever this happened it would fuel me with a new lease of life and cast away any negativity.

Later in the afternoon, a car pulled into a lay-by in front of me and three excited passengers jumped out to greet me. They explained that they had heard my interview on the radio and decided to come out to meet me, along with a flask of hot chocolate and warm mince pies. I couldn't thank them enough for their kind words and generosity. For the rest of the day I felt so good because of this one kind act. They will never know what a tremendous boost to my morale they gave me.

By 5pm I had made the steep climb to the top of High Ham. Having run 40 miles I had reached the halfway point for that day and now had the return journey back home. It felt so good to reach the furthest point of the run slightly ahead of schedule.

Running back across a bleak deserted stretch of the Somerset Levels, it started to snow again, which looked worse in the beam of a headtorch. I found watching the huge snowflakes falling before me quite soothing and hypnotic as I ran into the silence of the night.

At Glastonbury I was glad to see two support runners, Jane and Tracey, who had come out unexpectedly to keep me company. They were a great help in keeping up my pace back to the Mendips, where I knew the road conditions would be at their worst.

The snow had now turned into very cold persistent rain which gradually started to seep through my jacket and leggings. It was now that I had to really concentrate to keep the dreaded fatigue at bay.

With the steep climb back up over the Mendips proving nearly impossible on the slippery ice, we managed to find a channel of water that ran down the side of the road which was the only area devoid of ice. We had no choice but to run in this as we could grip the surface beneath, but instantly our poor feet turned icy cold which proved to be very painful.

I was so glad to reach the Hunters Lodge in Priddy, when on opening the door to the pub we were instantly hit by the warmth of a coal fire from within. Removing my backpack, while trying my best not to tangle the tall flag in the pub's Christmas decorations, provided a good laugh for the regulars, but we were soon all settled and tucking into a hot dish of delicious cauliflower cheese that instantly gave us extra warmth.

For a while I sat mesmerised as I watched the flames leaping from the fire and absorbed the welcome heat that it radiated.

After discreetly changing my wet socks for the comfort of new dry ones, I replaced my trainers ready for the next 16-mile section back home. As I pushed my chair back under the table, I couldn't help but notice the large puddle of water underneath that had collected on the old slab stone floor, from the three weary travellers. After thanking Jane and Tracey for coming out to find me in such horrible conditions and for giving up their time, when they could have so easily stayed in a warm cosy home, I set off on my own again into the dark cold night for the long journey home.

The rain had now stopped and been replaced by a bitterly cold wind that relentlessly blew from the north. For the first time that day the skies now cleared, revealing the stunning star-filled heavens above, devoid of any light pollution on the top of the Mendips.

Black ice had now formed on the roads, which proved impossible to see until you came across it, then suddenly without warning lose all traction and go hurtling towards the grass verge!

I was greeted by my dogs as soon as I entered the front door at 3:30am. They were full of hugs and tail wagging and so excited to see me back. I found a note from the neighbours saying that the dogs had been on several long runs and wished me good luck for the following day. I gave them another quick run around the local streets to settle them down, before showering, putting the washing in and stocking up my backpack with fresh kit and supplies.

I decided not to go to bed but to snatch some sleep on the sofa instead. There would be only a couple of hours sleep during this three-hour break if I was lucky. The excitement of the run was vividly pumping through my veins! With the alarm set, I lay down with a blanket, surrounded by my faithful hounds, and eventually drifted into a deep sleep.

My alarm clock was very unforgiving as it rattled away from me across the floor, out of arms reach. I tried to lift my tired body off the sofa, but the weight of a huge springer spaniel with his paws stretched out fully in front of him across my chest prevented me from doing so! After about a minute of my alarm clock doing a full circuit of the living-room floor, Scooby, with his tail wagging, decided to release me, as he slowly slid to the floor to stretch and yawn simultaneously.

Slowly, I stood up and staggered into the kitchen to make a pot of tea that I hoped would perform a miracle on my tired old body. It didn't matter how hard I tried to shake off the overwhelming sense of tiredness, it just wouldn't leave me.

Keeping a sharp eye on the time, that was passing by at an

alarming rate, I took the dogs for a quick walk before leaving a note thanking the neighbours. As I set off on the second day's circuit at a slower pace than the previous day, and still feeling uncomfortably tired, I had a phone call from some support runners who were waiting for me just up the road ahead.

It felt really good to run with them. They set a good pace which was certainly faster than if I had been running on my own.

Having good conversation with everyone seemed to pull me out of my state of tiredness and refocus me on the event.

Overnight a lot of the snow and ice had disappeared from the Mendip Hills, making my route so much easier to negotiate. Throughout the day I had continuous support, where many of the runners said that they were glad to come out and join me and lose some of the over-indulgence of Christmas!

After completing another long climb to the top of High Ham, I got everything ready in preparation for running through another night. I was joined by Ian who helped me increase my pace and pull the schedule back on track before reaching the furthest point on the circuit at Othery. Having to climb back up to the top of High Ham, Ian looked at me with a smile, then commented that he should have waited until I had passed, so he wouldn't have had to climb the hill.

Fourteen miles later, Ian left me at Glastonbury where I met Jane and Tracey again. I remarked to them that they looked a lot drier than when I had last seen them the previous evening. If it had started to rain while they were out with me again, I don't think that I would have ever been forgiven!

For the last ten miles I had kept a look out for my nephew Joe, who had phoned to arrange to bring out a hot drink for me. While running out of Glastonbury we came to a large roundabout where, perched on the top of one of the traffic islands, there was a large flask of coffee with a note attached. "To Uncle John, please enjoy. Sorry that I couldn't find you". While enjoying the fresh coffee as the night began to get colder, I gave Joe a call to thank him. It's small things like this that make each event so much more enjoyable. Every time I now pass through Glastonbury, I remember the flask stood on top of the roundabout traffic island.

At 2am, I said goodbye to Jane and Tracey and thanked them for joining me once again. I had now run 140 miles in the two-day period and was about to achieve my highest continuous mileage to date.

I felt really tired as the early hours and all the miles began to take their toll. Fighting sleep deprivation seemed to be the hardest issue. All too easily I felt as though I could have slept while standing still. On my own, it was a very long and wet 20-mile journey back over the Mendip Hills to reach home once again.

Exhausted, wet and very sore, I managed to make it home at 7am, having covered 160 miles in two days. Physically and mentally it had taken everything I had to give. I had now run 20 miles further than ever before, and still had the option of running another day, if only I could pull together enough strength and determination.

I immediately had a really hot shower, and stood there allowing the steaming hot water to drive the chill from my body. It felt so good to change into freshly washed clothes after being in the same cold wet running gear all day. The new clothes revealed all the sore areas around my body, sustained by the constant movement of wet garments rubbing against exposed skin.

With no time to lose I had to quickly regain my thoughts and concentrate on what I was doing. First of all, I sat down for a quick meal and rehydrated with several cups of tea, before taking my dogs out for a quick walk around their favourite circuit. This also allowed me to stretch out my legs and release some of the lactic acid that had built up.

I tried to catch a few hours sleep, but found myself constantly waking up in a state of panic to check the time and make sure that I hadn't overslept.

Finally, I decided that it was going to be impossible to go to sleep.

Even though my body felt so tired, my mind would not settle and constantly hounded me about the multitude of tasks that I needed to complete within the next hour in order to do my last run.

I tried as hard as possible to make a decision about what the final days mileage would be, but the harder I tried to concentrate, the more tired I became.

In desperation, I poured myself a really strong coffee and made a decision using the timetables in front of me to attempt to run 65 miles that day, if my body would let me.

It would have been so easy to have convinced myself that I had already run 20 miles further than I had ever run before, and call it a day! But it would have haunted me to have just given up and thrown the opportunity away.

Just then my phone rang; it was a local radio station wondering if I could give a live interview from Radstock town centre. With only half an hour to spare I got all my kit together and was on my way to meet them.

Taking part in the live interview helped me forget a lot of the aches and pains that I had been battling with earlier. Instead, I now concentrated on achieving my last goal of running another 65 miles.

Completing circuits on a daily basis has both advantages and disadvantages. The advantages being that you know your route without too much navigation; it's easier for support runners to find you locally; and it's much simpler with regards to timetables and planning. The main disadvantage is that you know how much some parts of the circuit are going to hurt, especially when you have ascents like the Mendip Hills to contend with.

Four hours later I had covered another 20 miles and now had help from several support runners along the way who, with their banter, were a great distraction from all the aches and pains and kept me alert and on schedule.

By midnight I had reached High Ham, which was my furthest point out and over halfway through my intended schedule. I had now covered 198 miles and was on my final journey home.

The sky was really clear and filled with stars that pierced the darkness of the night with flickers of light. There was complete silence on the deserted country lanes apart from a lone owl warning me away from its territory.

I could feel the temperature drop in the early hours of the morning, my warm breath would form small clouds as it hit the cold air in the beam of my headtorch.

Quickly, I changed into some warmer items of clothing. I found simple things like replacing the backpack a struggle as the straps twisted awkwardly on my arms. Then starting off again and maintaining a good pace was the biggest problem.

Climbing some of the smaller slopes became a real chore as my tired legs refused to regain full momentum, and I staggered sideways as I ran along the pavements. This gradually got worse as my mind screamed at me to stop and sleep.

As I slowly reached the top of Glastonbury High Street at 5:30am, I reluctantly walked into a bus shelter to sit down and rest. I poured the remainder of a cup of lukewarm stale coffee from my flask. It tasted foul, but was warm and wet, as I convinced myself that it would be enough to see me through the next six miles, until I reached Wells. About ten minutes later, I woke up with the sensation of something slapping against my face. Jumping to my feet, not knowing for a while where I was, I finally came to my senses as I realised my backpack had slid to the floor and the flag had been fluttering away in the breeze, gently brushing against my face.

With tired limbs, I ran along the lonely stretch of road that led into Wells, looking desperately for anywhere that sold coffee in the early hours of the morning. I eventually gave up and had to settle for a cold can of drink along with several bars of chocolate from a newsagent.

Daylight had now broken, as I clumsily walked up through the old market place, struggling to remove the stubborn wrappers from the chocolate bars. Giving up trying to multitask I sat down in the corner of the Penniless Porch which leads through to the Cathedral Green. With heavy eyes I took shelter from the freezing chill that swept up through the open streets and rested once more while slowly grazing on my snacks.

I was woken up a while later by a man pulling a noisy rubbish cart over the cobbles in front of me. I remembered checking the schedule when I arrived in Wells and saw that I was exactly on time. But now, 30 minutes had passed! Having completely fallen asleep, I must have looked like a tramp sleeping on the side of the pavement!

Embarrassed, I hurriedly did a final kit check and scampered out of Wells to make my last ascent of the Mendip Hills.

Soon I was joined by several runners who had brought out a fresh flask of coffee along with several other snacks. With new support I quickly made up the lost time and thrashed the final seven miles around Chew Valley Lake, before an unbelievable sprint finish at the Prince of Waterloo pub in Winford.

We had covered 225 miles in three days and five hours; 85 miles further than I had ever run before. Never would I have believed that I would have been capable of running eight-and-a-half marathons back to back.

I had learnt so much from this latest run regarding what the human body is capable of and coping with major factors like sleep deprivation, lack of nutrition and the effects that weather conditions can impose on you.

***

The following day, I saw in my local newspaper that I had been voted second place in the 'People of the Year' award in the local community. This was a fantastic way to end 2010 and made all the months of training and organisation seem worthwhile.

One of the comments that I frequently had after finishing my multiday events would be: "I bet you couldn't wait to have a decent night's sleep?" In reality this never happened. After being out on the road for over three days and having pushed my body to its limit, I had to learn to relax gradually over a period of time rather than come to an immediate halt, which would risk organ damage or failure. After the three day event, I would go to bed and set my alarm for only three hours. Then I would get up and take my dogs out for a two mile jog before going back to sleep, then do the same thing all over again.

The worst tiredness usually came two days after the event, when my body finally relaxed and believed that I wasn't going to ask the impossible from it again.

One of the other things I found was that, as I constantly chased a strict timetable on my events, I would be pushing myself through enormous waves of fatigue. I would argue with my body when it just wanted to stop. So once the event was over there was nothing for my mind to chase.

After landing back into a calm relaxed environment once more, it felt at times that I had withdrawal symptoms from the run. This was usually the time when I started planning the next adventure!

Within a week of my last event, I had a secret plan to run a 300-mile event! Would this be possible or was I just massively out of my depth in terms of reality?

Night after night, after finishing work I would think through all the possibilities, studying my last event timetable for hours on end, recalling both good and bad memories.

In my last event I had run approximately 80 miles for the first two days and 65 for the last, over a circuit that was far from easy in terms of the total amount of ascent en route. If only I could squeeze another 75-mile day of running on top of the last run and achieve the amazing 300-mile target!

It was a warm sunny January morning as I drove with Bob to another meeting with the CHSW fundraising team. As usual I loved meeting the care teams, as well as the main fundraising organisation who always came out to see me during my visits.

At the meeting I was told that we had now raised a staggering total of £35,000 over the last few years. I immediately thought back to the Bristol half marathon, which was my first fundraising event for them. Never could I have envisaged raising anywhere near that sum of money back then.

After continuously raising money year after year, I found it difficult to approach those who knew me for sponsorship, so I posted a fundraising page on a website which the media very kindly promoted on my behalf.

While I was at the meeting, I mentioned in conversation that I intended to attempt running 300 miles, over a four-day period. At first there was a look of total disbelief followed by an unnerving silence around the room, as everyone cautiously looked at each other. To break the tension I quickly explained my account of the 225-mile run and what a success it had been despite the awful weather conditions. I added that I planned to run from Land's End to Bath Abbey, incorporating the new hospice, Little Harbour, that was being built in Porthpean, and while passing, hold a press interview to highlight its importance to Cornwall.

Then, before anyone could say anything else, I quickly spread several maps across the conference table with my route brightly highlighted across each.

Slowly everyone turned their attention away from the maps and focused on me, as I sat there like a huge Cheshire cat! The team never knew what to expect from me at any of our meetings, but I was sure this event would attract a lot of awareness and hopefully funding to promote their good work.

In order to give myself plenty of time to finalise the route and timetable, the event was planned for 26th – 30th May. This would also give me a reasonable amount of daylight and hopefully better weather conditions.

Another advantage I had with this run was that I already had a route and timetable from the previous year, all the way from the Tamar bridge back up to Radstock.

With Paddo for company I drove around exploring the whole of Cornwall over the next couple of weekends. We soon became familiar with all the small coves and country lanes that led from Land's End up to the Tamar Bridge, plus all the delicious bakeries.

One day, after introducing Paddo to the Pacific Ocean at one of the small coves, (he had never seen such a big pond before!) we found an amazing little bakery. After sampling some of the products, we decided to buy six large pasties with the intention of them lasting a few days. In reality they didn't even make the journey home!

Rather than enter organised events, I now focused my attention on planning my own routes, as I found planning and exploring interesting new trails really enjoyable.

The months seemed to pass really quickly, especially when I still worked long hours, training whenever I could and giving various charity talks.

I always knew when I had to increase my training, because my body would start to show signs of the dreaded seizures returning.

With the month of May fast approaching, I organised two longer runs in April. The first was a route I put together which would take me on a trail around three local reservoirs, covering a tough 40-mile circuit.

The three lakes run, Sunday 10th April, 2011

The cool early morning breeze swept over the ridges of the Mendip Hills along with the sun's golden rays, lighting up droplets of dew that hung delicately from each blade of grass like tiny jewels.

Starting at Charterhouse adventure centre, opposite the quaint little church that stands alone overlooking the picturesque valley of Velvet Bottom, I set off through the remains of the old Roman lead mines, then followed footpaths that lead me across open fields.

About six miles on, while descending from the Mendip Hills on steep grassy slopes overlooking East and West Harptree, I had the opportunity to fully appreciate the magnificent views of the rolling valleys that neatly held Chew Valley Lake in their grasp.

Great childhood memories came flooding back as I passed New Manor Farm at North Widcombe, where the hillsides in spring would be covered in magnificent carpets of primroses. I wasn't disappointed as I passed the steep sloped fields to find them looking just as beautiful again, if not more impressive, with their fine blooms shining in the bright sunshine overlooking Chew Valley Lake.

At 18 miles I had completed the climb up out of the valley, on the opposite side of where I had been only hours before. Arriving in Nempnett Thrubwell I enjoyed my last spectacular view of Chew Valley Lake. Ahead and below me in the valley lay the deep blue waters of Blagdon Lake, surrounded by pockets of lush green trees around its shores. After climbing many steep hills on narrow country lanes, the dam and pumping station at the far end of Blagdon Lake soon appeared. As I made my way up into Blagdon village, I was soon drawn into one of the local pubs by the magnificent smell of cooked dinners coming from within.

"What, no chips on the menu?" I thought to myself, as I frantically scanned it from front to back one more time. "No, no chips" said the landlady, "but we can serve you a large bowl of roast potatoes."

After enjoying a short break which included a massive bowl of roast potatoes and a pint of refreshing beer, I scanned the maps once more to double check the route for the second half of the run.

With my supplies replenished, I was soon heading over Beacon Batch, the highest point of the Mendip Hills. With the view of Blagdon Lake now fast disappearing behind me in the hot midday sun, I descended the steep rocky slopes into Cheddar.

The reservoir was very busy with people enjoying the fine weather. The lack of footpath signs, along with the unfamiliar countryside, made the run at this point frustrating. A constant stream of sweat now trickled into my eyes, which made reading the maps almost impossible. After stopping for a brief while to refocus my attention on the run and check my navigation, I soon found my way through a maze of small fields which eventually led out onto a narrow lane leading to the small secluded village of Nyland.

Here, I came across a tiny sign indicating 'Farm shop ahead', so I quickened the pace in the hope of finding a nice cool drink before it shut. But as I ran around the corner I found another sign saying 'Farm shop open last Saturday of every month'. My heart dropped.

Draycott and the cliffs of Cheddar were as unforgiving as ever, but the views never ceased to amaze me. After crossing the top of Cheddar Gorge, Velvet Bottom felt very comfortable to run up, with its soft texture underfoot after all the hard rock and stone tracks previously encountered.

Very soon the little church at Charterhouse came back into view after a long, hot, but very satisfying run. I found a whole new level of contentment running these local trails, and exploring so many hidden places and beautiful countryside that I would never have otherwise seen – these were truly Somerset's hidden jewels.

My second run at the end of April would incorporate both trail and road over a 40-mile circuit which would take me from Aust Service Station on the M48 in England across the Severn bridge into Wales and back again.

Severn Bridge run, Sunday 24th April, 2011

The huge white structure of the Severn Bridge towered before me as I ran from Aust service station along the footpath that travels alongside the M48 into Wales.

At 7am my legs felt really tired, but soon loosened up from the previous day's hard 21-mile run, along part of the Monarchs Way between Compton Martin and Pylle.

Having driven over the bridge several times, I really appreciated the views that it had to offer crossing it on foot. A gentle breeze that circulated up from the River Severn below felt most welcome as the sun rose into the clear morning sky, growing ever stronger.

Two miles later I was following a narrow footpath running parallel to the River Wye, which led through quiet back streets before entering onto fields that harboured a multitude of items deposited by the high spring tides. From here I followed ancient tracks that wound themselves through sheltered woods, until I came to the old fort wall that once guarded the town of Chepstow.

Making my way down through the old narrow streets, I soon came upon Chepstow Castle, with its huge stone structure proudly standing out from the surrounding hillside. After several miles of running up through the Wye Valley I stopped at one of the many viewpoints overlooking the River Wye, admiring it, as it twisted its way down through the valley below, with the castle and Severn Bridge in the distant background.

While running back across the bridge, I was suddenly joined by a huge hairy fairy, complete with sparkling wand!

At this point I became very worried. Had I overdone all the running? Was this a mirage that appeared on the bridge to haunt exhausted travellers?

The silence was quickly broken as they asked me, in a really gruff voice, if it was okay to join me on my run back to Aust. I later found out that it was one of the local lads from the nearby army barracks, out on a charity run. He certainly attracted a lot of attention from passing motorists, wearing a short see-through skirt and make-up. I couldn't help thinking it must have been pretty draughty with the cool sea breeze, but good on him for raising money for a breast cancer charity.

Once back at Aust, I departed from the fairy to run on my own, over the same circuit again. But this time I went on further as I couldn't resist following above the River Wye, seeing the stunning forests lined with bluebells.

On returning back to Chepstow Castle, I saw a sign saying cream teas. It was the perfect excuse for me to stop; after all, I had done a few extra miles, it was hot, and there were a lot of hills… OK, I was going in there anyway!

On closer inspection while inside, I found a whole raspberry Victoria sponge cake, totally untouched. Quickly I asked the lady behind the counter how much it cost.

She replied that it was £1.50 a slice and would I like a piece? Wondering what kind of reaction she would give me, I replied, "I want to buy the whole cake please!"

After a few seconds of silence and with a fixed gaze she asked me if I was being serious. When she saw that I was, she disappeared into the kitchen and came back with the café owner.

After explaining to her how much I enjoyed delicious home cooking and that I was on an intensive training run for my 300-mile event the following month, she agreed to sell me the whole cake and a pot of tea for a very generous £10!

Minutes later, while seated in a sunny garden with fine views out onto the castle, I was joined by my cake and a large pot of tea, enough to make a king feel really proud. For the next 30 minutes I sat in the tranquillity of the garden and watched the world go by, while carving away several large slices of cake.

My silence was broken by the inquisitive owner, asking if I would like any more tea to drink, which I never refuse. She then commented on the empty cake stand and couldn't believe that I had eaten the entire cake. With a nervous and almost unbelieving smile, she returned with another pot of tea, before leaving me to enjoy.

On leaving, I couldn't thank her enough for looking after me and she wished me good luck for my run in May.

It took a while to pick up the pace once again with such a full belly, but I was soon back on form and counting all the towers on the bridge as I passed under them, on my way back to Aust.

CROSSING THE COUNTIES

The following three weeks passed so quickly. I had been asked so many times if I felt nervous about taking on the 300-mile challenge, but in all honesty, with so much to organise, I didn't have any spare time left to think about it.

As with all my long runs, a new sense of excitement began to fill me during the final couple of days leading up to the event. I couldn't wait to get started and grasp the challenge with both hands to prove that it could be done.

My heart would pound away with the excitement of the enormous challenge ahead of me, especially the thought of running eleven marathons back to back, while burning 36,000 calories. Only a year ago I completed 140 miles, now I would be doubling that distance as I entered into unknown territory once more.

300-mile run: Thursday 26th-30th May, 2011

Travelling down to Land's End on 26th May with Bob and Viv, I had plenty of time to go through the previous eight months of planning that had gone into this latest adventure.

With the wind and rain lashing down on the car, I was more than grateful to be inside and not yet out on the 300-mile run. I couldn't help thinking of little Paddo sat in the front window, who I had left a few hours earlier. I bet he thought, "the old man's gone a long time getting his paper this morning."

As I walked across the car park in Land's End the sun had now come out, highlighting the rugged coastline and the huge waves that came crashing up and over the rocky cliff face, carried by a strong gale off the Atlantic.

With an hour still to go until the start of the run, it felt good to relax with cups of tea and have time to stroll around and study the distant shorelines that I would soon be travelling past.

After triple checking all my kit and supplies, I had everything broken-down and sorted for each day, and my equipment ready to hand for when it was needed.

It was now 5pm, time to start. My goal was to reach Bath Abbey, some 300 miles and 96 hours away. With Bob, Viv and two members of the CHSW friends group counting down the last few seconds, the run was finally under way and for the first time I found myself facing the reality of this ambitious challenge.

The Cornish countryside offered many fascinating features that only seemed to reveal themselves when walking, or in our case running, through its narrow country lanes. The Merry Maid stone circles are a good example of such a feature, that appeared in a quiet secluded field as we passed. The only noise that I could hear at this point were the skylarks flying overhead, as they enjoyed the evening sun, which cast magical shadows beyond each of the stones.

At this point we had passed three miles, which I felt very pleased with, until I realised this meant we had covered only 1% of the entire run. This thought was soon cast away as my concentration was quickly diverted to spotting wild flowers in the hedgerows, especially the edible ones!

Running down the quiet narrow streets of Mousehole, the small fishing harbour appeared before us. Waiting patiently there were Andy, Sue, Andrea and Fiona, from Hale Running club, who kindly arranged to meet and escort me round the coast to Marazion. It felt good to have company and to share experiences with fellow runners who quickly pointed out special places of interest along the way.

As we ran along the seafront in Penzance, Viv suddenly handed me a huge portion of fish and chips. They were gratefully received and promptly disappeared by the time we ran into Marazion, much to the amazement of the Hale runners who had never witnessed anyone consume such a meal while running.

St Michael's Mount looked magnificent as the sun gently set down behind it, silhouetting the grand structure against the sea.

Sadly, the Hale Running club team now departed. I missed their company, as we made our way inland to the villages of Goldsithney and Godolphin Cross. It was now 10pm and time to prepare to run through the long hours of the night.

At midnight we passed through Helston and on into Constantine, after travelling up and down every hill that Cornwall could throw at us. Every now and then we caught a glimpse of the incredible view of Falmouth Harbour in the distance, which was brightly lit up in an array of magnificent colours that pierced the night sky.

I watched as the thousands of stars gradually disappeared, one by one from the heavens, as we entered a new day. During all the time I had been out running so far, Bob and Viv had either ran with me, or driven the difficult route, providing flasks of coffee along the way.

Falmouth was now proudly displaying Pendennis Castle as we entered the grand harbour. Unfortunately, Rick Stein's famous establishment was closed at 5am – I shall have to have a word with him!

Penryn and Carnon Downs soon came into view. The King Harry Ferry must be around the next corner! Several hills and many corners later, there it was. The ferryboat was gently making its way to the far side of the shore, surrounded in a peaceful morning mist.

Wasting no time, the kettle was soon whistling away on the stove and spoiling me with a fresh brew of tea. I rapidly tucked into breakfast as the King Harry Ferry faithfully returned, ready for us to continue our journey across the river Fal.

Heading inland, encountering more relentless hills, we needed a distraction from the amount of ascent and descent that was constantly taking place. So along with some help from Viv, I decided to guess an alternative meaning for all the signs displaying B&B. The best that we could come up with was 'badger and beans' – desperate times indeed!

At Pendower Beach the road suddenly disappeared where coastal erosion had made its presence felt. The surrounding beaches and coves looked so calm sheltering the turquoise sea in their laps. Again, all you could hear were the native birds enjoying the morning sun, along with the gentle waves lapping against the golden sands.

After stopping for a pasty at the unspoilt fishing harbour of Mevagissey, the road to Porthpean proved relentless with its steep climbs. They say that beauty comes at a price, and with such views, it was well worth it. With the sun beaming from a clear blue sky we soon arrived, slightly ahead of schedule, at Little Harbour – the new children's hospice in Porthpean.

The hospice was near completion and the whole area felt special with its views of the surrounding countryside in one direction and a commanding view over St Austell bay to the other. After twenty-one-and-a-half hours of non-stop running we had completed 87 miles of unforgettable countryside with enough beautiful scenery to last a lifetime.

After a refreshing shower, change of kit, good food and a short nap, Bob, Viv and myself were back on the road once again making our way out of St Austell.

After an hour-and-a-half of non-stop hill climbing we finally arrived at Cathew. Through the still, clear evening we could see, far in the distance, the lights of Bodmin and several little villages tucked into the valleys around us.

As we entered into the village of Roach, I could just make out the eerie shape of St Michael's Chapel and Hermitage, high on the top of Roach Rock, silhouetted against the night sky.

Passing under the A30 at 2:30am, I couldn't help but notice how it was still so busy with all the Bank Holiday traffic. A smile came to my face as I thought of all the people arriving in Cornwall – I bet that none of them would be running back home!

The stillness and silence of the night was suddenly illuminated by the flashing blue lights of a police patrol car that had just pulled over our support car. Just as I was thinking, "here we go again, B&B in a cell!", the officers began praising us for our fundraising efforts. It felt really good to be recognised in the middle of the countryside. Our effort now seemed a lot more worthwhile at such an unsociable hour.

Feeling so tired, that I was on the verge of sleep running, I sat in the front seat of Viv's car and had a really deep sleep for 15 minutes, before grappling with my backpack and continuing with the run.

I found that snatching sleep in this way was far more beneficial than trying to programme sleep breaks, where you try and force yourself to sleep at a given time. Power-naps for this length of time also prevented the build-up of lactic acid which can occur during longer rest periods.

Daylight gently made its entrance through the darkness to reveal a cool, damp Bodmin Moor, where the skylarks welcomed us with their songs through the country lanes.

On reaching Bolventor, we turned around at the famous Jamaica Inn and continued towards Liskeard. The drizzle had now started to come in much harder than before as did the tiredness of the early morning and 36 hours of continuous hills.

On approaching Liskeard I started to feel really exhausted. It didn't matter how much I tried to increase my pace, another hill would intrude and deflate my enthusiasm, time and time again.

I felt really sad to see Bob leave to catch his train back to Bath, but I was joined by Kevin and Martyn who were good company and helped set a fresh pace through all the hilly lanes around Liskeard.

Saltash seemed to take forever to arrive. Because of the slower pace I now had the additional problem of lactic acid building up in the top of my legs. This proved to be extremely painful, especially on the hills. While focused on my stretching programme to try and relieve the pain, my running pace reduced further, which resulted in my time dropping well behind schedule.

Looking up at the towers of the Tamar bridge was a temporary distraction. I felt a reassurance reaching one of my favourite landmarks, but at the same time tried to ignore the fact that I had never been so far behind on a scheduled run.

As we approached Smeaton's Tower, the huge lighthouse on Plymouth Hoe, we were asked if we had come to join the local fun run that was being held that day around the city!

From here I departed from Kevin and Martyn to run solo on to Marsh Mills, with Viv faithfully following in the support car.

The time was now 8pm and I should have been ten miles further on, stopping for my next intended break. But here I was, two-and-a-half-hours late, with a ten-mile constant uphill climb to the edge of Dartmoor ahead of me.

It was a dark, wet and sombre evening. Feeling broken and shattered with legs that were so painful, I sank down and sat on the roadside kerb, with my feet in the gutter, not even noticing the stream of water passing over the top of them. I grasped my hands firmly over my face trying to hide my tears from Viv.

I sat for a moment in a state of despair searching for the best option. Should I have an extra-long unplanned break now and carry on tomorrow? This would put even more strain and mileage onto day three. After all I had covered 157 miles, which is further than I had ran in last year's 140-mile event. I knew if I did make this decision I would be giving in to the biggest mental and physical demons I had ever encountered. This would not have helped me with the rest of the run. In fact it would have led to the failure of the event, which wasn't an option after eight long months of preparation.

Shuffling up from the kerb, I climbed unsteadily to my feet and with all my energy managed to limp unceremoniously into a local takeaway situated behind me, then devour a triple burger, bag of salty fries and a large bottle of fizzy drink.

Wearily, I told Viv in the support car that I was going to complete the ten mile section up to Yelverton and that I would meet him there in the car park next to the café. This section was all off-road and not possible to drive. I told him that if I had any problems I promised to phone him immediately, as the worried look on his face confirmed how bad I felt!

Breaking from a very painful shuffle into a slight jog I started the ascent on the off-road section. Every muscle felt as though it was going to burst. Gradually I lengthened each stride and soon increased my pace. Remembering all the good wishes and support from everyone, along with the vivid conversations with parents and care staff from CHSW, provided me with all the strength that was needed at this crucial moment.

Quickening the pace ever more, the aches and pains melted into a distant memory and the miles now passed as they should have done earlier.

At 10am, I arrived in Yelverton car park feeling like a new person. I now felt as happy and fresh as I had done on day one, with all traces of the problems that I had encountered ten miles earlier having gone. Viv looked so happy and relieved to see me arrive in good time. It was time for the tea and cake to come out of hiding.

To come through so much negativity and now feel on top of the world was indescribable. I could lose a couple of rest breaks and be back on schedule.

Approaching 11:40pm it was great to see Jane, Julia and Tracey arrive in their support car to take over from the outstanding support Viv had given me. After transferring all the kit I was off running with the ladies over Dartmoor. The moors took on a sinister character, as relentless rain and gusts of wind lashed out at us.

I felt very grateful for all the support I had been given: Viv, who had been with me for two-and-a-half days, Bob for two, and everyone else who had come so far to join me. And now the ladies, who were taking it in turns to run with me across Dartmoor in atrocious weather conditions in the middle of the night.

At 3am I felt tired enough to drop, so climbing into the front seat of Julia's car, I barely had time to put my head inside of the door before I was fast asleep.

Fifteen minutes later, we were pounding the roads once again and heading up yet another hill over Dartmoor.

The storms and wind had now departed as daybreak emerged through the last of the heavy clouds. One by one the birds began to join in singing another beautiful dawn chorus. I commented to the ladies how peaceful and quiet the countryside was as we left the moors, then we were interrupted by a cuckoo at 4:45am. Half-an-hour later it was still going strong somewhere in the distant trees, as though in defiance of what I had just said!

In order to keep a constant pace, I was having regular breaks to maintain high levels of food intake along with stretching to reduce lactic acid. I was now only one hour behind my schedule instead of two-and-a-half the previous day.

While giving a live radio interview on my phone, miles away in both thoughts and conversation, Jane suddenly made me aware of a very large and irate bull who was only a few metres behind me. Foaming at the mouth and stomping his feet into the ground, all that separated us was a flimsy wire fence. So, deciding that I didn't want to increase my running pace, I sauntered off out of sight around the corner, taking my flag with me!

En route we met so many interesting people who wanted to know what we were doing, or had heard about us from the local radio stations. One fellow even stopped on a bike ride from John o' Groats to Land's End to support us.

Climbing the Blackdown Hills seemed easier than any time I had run them before, as regular stretching had resulted in no more acid building up.

As I entered Churchinford everything felt really good and my body was holding out well, considering that it had just covered 230 miles – the furthest I had ever run before.

Pat and Chris, along with my old school friend Dave Clark, joined me to take over the support driving. At 1am, after a quick ten minute power nap, we left through the dead of night, escorted by the support cars.

High Ham now stood towering before us as daylight began to part the night sky, its huge southern slope looking every bit as menacing as it had done so many times before. Reaching the church that stands so peacefully on the top of the hill, I had now passed so many of the dreaded hills and tried to blank out the other three still to come. Anyway, I had decided at the start of the run that there were no hills, only undulations that were there to be conquered!

Entering Wells at 7:30am, I thanked the runners for joining me through the night then quickly snatched another ten minutes sleep in the front of Dave's car. This time I managed to run up all the steep hill that leads out of Wells to reach the Hunter's Lodge Pub in Priddy. It felt so good to see friends who had come out in the rain to support me for the final 25 miles.

Leaning against the back of Dave's car in my own little world, with a thousand-and-one things running through my mind, I looked down to see little Paddo rushing up on his lead to join me. Reaching down he immediately jumped up into my arms and gave me the biggest hug ever. Time had passed so quickly; I hadn't seen the little fellow for four days after leaving him with Richard and Vicky who had now come to join me for the 15-mile run back to Radstock.

With Chris driving in front of all the runners in the leading support car, I could see Paddo stood on the passenger seat, constantly watching me in the rear view mirror.

Midsomer Norton Rugby Club welcomed us with hot drinks and the chance to warm up inside the clubhouse, away from the icy cold conditions.

Looking up at my cousin Phil's photograph that hung amongst so many others in the club, it was hard thinking that nearly four years had passed since losing him. As I got ready to leave with some more support runners, I could vividly recall Phil's voice saying "call yourself a runner?" with that contagious smile of his.

The mile-long hill out of Radstock presented no problems to us as we took it with pace, with the eagerness to finish being felt by all. Dunkerton Hill was the last really steep hill that stood between us and the finish in Bath. This again was taken at such a quick pace that we had to stop at the top and lose some time! At the rate we were going we would arrive in Bath an hour ahead of schedule and before all the people we were going to meet had got there. I could see no choice but to have a picnic in the lay-by – another excuse for tea and cake!

Sprinting up through the main shopping precinct in Bath to cross the finish line in front of the Abbey felt remarkably good, as my dream became a reality.

Standing amongst all the supporters who had gathered in the Abbey churchyard, I looked up at three massive inflatable balloons displaying '300'. It was then that the enormity of the run finally hit me. I suddenly felt really emotional as I reflected back over the last 95 hours. We had completed 300 miles in well under four days, had time for a picnic on the way in, ran in just about every weather condition including fog, rain, gale force winds and sunshine. We also saw the sun rise four times while out on the same run, and survived on just five hours sleep!

I felt so proud that I had been given so much time and support from my fellow runners and friends, during, and leading up to, the 300-mile run. Their belief in what I was doing and my reasons for doing it had kept me focused when times got really difficult. They were my strength when I needed it most.

With all my running kit safely in the washing machine, I managed to soak for an hour in a scalding hot bath, as I reflected back over the run, recapturing so many special memories.

A lot of the runners who had joined me had unintentionally run further than they had ever before, having been caught up in the amazing atmosphere. The contagious banter certainly helped distract everyone from the mileage.

Very often after a long run, I am asked what the hardest moments had been. They wouldn't believe me when I told them it was actually after I had finished.

Multiple times during my sleep I would wake up in a state of panic thinking that I had slept through a huge section of my running timetable. I would then spend several minutes trying to figure out where I was, before realising that the run was now over and I was back in the comfort of my own home.

I found that the body usually takes two to three days to settle down to normality and that it was usually the second day after an event that it would reveal any damage, amongst all the normal aches and pains.

The sense of always being part of a magnificent team that included complete strangers we had met over the last four days, was absolutely priceless, but difficult to adjust to when back at home surrounded by silence on my own.

A month later, while attending a meeting with the CHSW team at Charlton Farm to help organise one of their Midnight Memory walks around Bristol, I was informed that I had now raised over £50,000 for their charity.

I was then further rewarded by several letters that they gave me from listeners of local radio stations, who had written in with their own personal donations and kind words of support for me.

***

As I now missed running in a larger group on my ultra-events, I decided to organise some weekend runs varying from 10–20 miles, which would allow people to join me for all or part of the run, depending on their strength and ability.

But more than anything I wanted it to be a good social event that people could enjoy while still being able to train and improve on their running.

The weekend runs proved very popular, covering new areas on road and exploring hidden trails across the incredible countryside that I'm so fortunate to have around me.

Very soon I found that a large number of the group were running further than they had before and setting themselves new goals in terms of mileage which was so good to see. Although the runs weren't particularly easy, they were enjoyable with all the banter that we had along with the breathtaking scenery. Little did I know at the time that this would be the foundation of my own running group, Westfield TT.

After the successful completion of my 300-mile run, I found new opportunities opening up for me. Local schools were now emailing me asking if I could give a talk to their pupils and other charities were inviting me to give advice to their runners entering full and half marathon events.

Despite feeling apprehensive about giving talks to schools, I agreed to visit St Cuthbert's School in Wells one morning.

As I began to talk to the children during their assembly, all my fears disappeared and were replaced by the enthusiasm of wanting to tell my story. At times you could have heard a pin drop as they were so quiet, then at others the teachers would look nervously back at me as the children erupted in laughter.

As with all my talks, I found that the time passed so quickly, I didn't have the chance to feel nervous about how it was going to work out. After each session I gave the children a chance to ask me questions, which I always found interesting, especially with the younger primary school pupils.

Some of the questions I have been asked include: "have you ever been chased by crocodiles or bears?"

"Can you run faster than a train?"

"When you run overnight do you worry about being chased by

monsters?"

Usually about a week after my talks, I would receive hand written cards from the pupils with their drawings on the front thanking me for visiting their school. I still have possession of each and every one of them which I find absolutely priceless, and every now and then I look back through them whenever I doubt myself over any challenge.

A RELAY TO REMEMBER

With Britain hosting the Olympic games in 2012, excitement and ambitions in all sporting activities seemed to increase. The enthusiasm and awareness around that time was a great benefit whenever I gave my talks. It helped promote the message of the importance of being fit and healthy and inspire people with what could be achieved through one's ambition.

In early August, after returning home from work one evening, I casually opened my laptop to check my emails before having to dash out for another training session with Wells running club. To my astonishment, I found that I had received four emails from the 2012 Olympic torch relay team. Nervously I opened each to find that I had my name put forward by different representatives to carry the Olympic torch!

At first, I couldn't believe what I was reading and thought that it must have been some sort of scam or joke, but when I checked out the website, I found it to be absolutely genuine and couldn't believe it was happening to me.

After reading the email several times, over and over again, I decided to print it off immediately in case it disappeared overnight!

Shaking with nerves, I accepted all four nominations and cautiously waited for the results to come back, which would be on 5th December 2011.

There were 12 regional selection panels who would be looking for individuals with the most inspirational stories. If successful, out of 2,800 nominations, they would be offered a place as one of the 8,000 torch bearers needed for the Olympic torch relay.

For the next few weeks I felt an incredible sense of excitement. I would wake each morning and convince myself that it had been a cruel dream, until I read the letter safely placed on my living room table once more.

It seemed a very long time until 5th December and throughout the four months of waiting I gradually prepared myself for the worst, as I doubted my chances of being so lucky to be part of this incredible event for the nation.

With the third Uphill to Wells relay race fast approaching, I wanted to do something special to mark the occasion. So, I decided to add an extra 20 miles on to last year's run which started in Bath.

After hours measuring various maps I decided I would start from the famous landmark of Bristol's Suspension Bridge. The route was just over 100 miles in total, starting at a venue everyone would recognise. My list of runs for this event now included:

- 1st run 2009: Wells – Uphill – Wells, 60 miles
- 2nd run 2010: Bath – Wells – Uphill – Wells, 80 miles
- 3rd run 2011: Bristol – Bath – Wells – Uphill – Wells, 100 miles.

Friday 23rd September, 2011

At 3pm, I was met by Kevin who had very kindly offered to drive me to Bristol for the start of my run. I was feeling lethargic after indulging in a huge dinner and struggling to even check my kit bag, let alone run 100 miles non-stop.

It was a warm and sunny afternoon as I left the splendour of Brunel's Suspension Bridge and made my way past several other famous landmarks that Bristol had to offer.

Just after I started my run at 4:30pm Radio Bristol rang me and asked if I would take part in a live interview to discuss my latest challenge, which I gladly accepted without hesitation.

After the interview the producer asked what route I would be taking as I made my way through the city and headed towards Bath. When I explained that I would be using the A4 – one of the busiest routes through the heart of Bristol – he asked if I would like to give out live traffic updates on air every 30 minutes, until 7pm!

After two hours of running, mostly alongside stationary traffic,

I arrived in Keynsham where I met up with some of my support runners. They immediately said that they heard me on the radio giving regular traffic reports, and wanted to know if I had acquired a new job.

It felt really good leaving all the traffic fumes behind me as I made my way out into the open countryside. At 8:30pm we arrived at Bath Abbey where the city was starting to get busy for Friday evening celebrations. From here I departed from the other runners and made the 10-mile journey back to my home in Westfield.

Quickly dashing through the front door, I swapped backpacks and made a flask of coffee to keep me alert overnight. It was important that I didn't waste any time while at home as I was on a tight schedule for the mileage.

Later, after arriving in Wells, my route on the West Mendip Way became a real challenge as a huge blanket of fog swept over the Mendip Hills and visibility dropped to only a few metres.

I found myself at times way off the trail, only to end up the wrong side of a forest or approaching unfamiliar buildings. Then I would have to retrace my steps back to a place of familiarity and start all over again. A lot of time was lost doing this, and the more tired I became, the harder it was to concentrate.

Gradually, as the first signs of daylight separated the fog from the darkness, navigation became easier, especially as I dropped down from the higher peaks into lower surrounding valleys where visibility was much better. By quickening my pace, I slowly regained my time and was back on schedule, which lifted my tired spirit.

With just over a mile to go until I reached the 70-mile point on Uphill beach, I had an unexpected phone call from Kevin informing me that he was waiting for me down on the beach with a flask of tea and bacon sandwiches. Suddenly my pace broke into a really fast run with the image of a delicious breakfast just ahead of me.

I couldn't thank Kevin enough for his kind support as I left Uphill for the final 30-mile section back to Wells. It was amazing support like this that made every one of my runs possible.

Knowing that the other teams would soon be following me, I concentrated hard on keeping a good pace. With 20 miles still to go, my legs began to feel the first signs of tiredness, along with a sore throat I had gained from the cold night air of the previous evening. While I had the chance, I purchased supplies from the only garage open on route and managed to reach Cheddar Gorge, before the first of the other runners caught up with me.

With the final five miles now in sight, I felt so close to the finish line, but found great difficulty descending the hundreds of steps which led through the beautiful scenery of Ebbor Gorge. My legs felt really tight and refused to bend without causing extreme agony. Several times I propped myself against a tree with one hand grasping hold of my ankle and attentively pulling my leg back as far as it would stretch towards my back. I repeated the procedure about ten times before moving on again, then did the same thing all over again just a few miles further on.

The sense of relief was immense as I crossed the finish line in the grounds of Wells Cathedral, after having ran twenty-five-and-a-half hours of both road and trail.

***

One problem I faced whenever I ran a half marathon was that people would say it was so easy for me, after running all my long-distance events.

I found running either distance difficult. With a half marathon I would run it as fast and hard as I could, then come over the finish line thoroughly exhausted and still took several days to recover.

This also made fundraising a lot harder. Unless I came up with a greater mileage for each run, people would comment "he's done that before" and would no longer be interested in sponsoring me.

Realising this, I decided to switch my attention slightly from running longer distances to teaching others to run faster and achieve their goals.

Weekends were the only time that I could spare to accommodate this new focus, but slowly, after several meetings I had my own little group of runners who wanted to train for marathon distances both on and off road.

The great benefit I found by training everyone as a group was that people didn't want to let each other down by not turning up for the training sessions. They also looked after each other and tended to progress at the same level. No one apart from myself would know the weekend route and every session would be different in terms of mileage, speed and elevation.

Weekend training demanded a lot of time and commitment, especially during bad weather or times when you just wanted to rest on a Sunday morning. But the rewards were priceless, seeing others achieve their goals and passing on all that I had learnt.

Even though I had still been running reasonable distances over the last two months since my 100-mile relay race in September, it was noticeable that my body was showing the first initial stages of shutting down again with the seizures coming back. With disturbed sleep patterns I needed to increase my mileage once more, to try and disperse the waste product from my body from past radiotherapy treatment.

After many hours of studying local maps, I came up with a 37-mile run which would include as many hills as possible. This would start at Brean Down and head over the Mendip Hills via a new route that I had never run, before finishing at a local pub which served great food.

Windmill Run, 11th November, 2011

As I arrived at Brean Down the sun shone brightly over the Bristol Channel as it reflected golden rays of light. A brisk cold wind greeted us from the North, as I met three other runners who had come along to accompany me at the start.

Although I had a backpack containing plenty of food and drink as well as spare clothing, I had purposely had very little to eat or drink that morning, to see how this would affect my running as the day progressed.

Leaving the car park, we then made the 97m climb to the top of Brean Down before running out to the furthest point that stretches out into the Bristol Channel. I always find the old Victorian fortress overlooking the sea most fascinating, especially the cannons that used to guard the shoreline.

After returning to the car park, we ran up the coastline passing Brean and Berrow sands, before departing inland at the lighthouse in Burnham-on-Sea.

On arriving at the base of Brent Knoll I departed from the other runners, who had to retrieve their cars, before making the steep 137m ascent to the top. Just as I thought I had made it to the top another ridge would appear, taking me up even further. Determined not to stop until I reached the top, I used my hands to assist my legs, pushing down hard on the top of each knee to help each stride.

We had covered a fast 11-mile route to reach the Knoll and my legs were absolutely stinging from the unforgiving ascent. The views from the top were incredible. Looking to the west you could see all the way across the Bristol Channel and over to Wales; to the east the Somerset Levels spread before you with the Mendip Hills in the background.

Feeling exhausted, I carried on with my journey back down over the south end of the Knoll before running through the hamlets of Vole and Chappel Allerton, where I snatched a quick break to admire the old windmill. I only consumed a small chocolate bar along with a mouthful of water to see what the effects would be on my body. Did I really need to consume as much as I had on previous long runs?

Very quickly I made my way through narrow country lanes and

across several interesting footpaths that led through farms, before reaching Nyland Hill at the foot of Draycott. The steep 76m climb to the top posed a real challenge on my tired legs, and by now I could feel the effects of hunger. Refusing at this stage to refuel, I ran on to reach Draycott, admiring all the autumn colours from the magnificent view that Nyland Hill had to offer.

After making the 261m ascent over the Mendip Hills, I reached much-welcomed level terrain that finally led into Priddy. Passing the local pub, I felt really tempted to go in and indulge in the fine ales and cuisine, but I knew I had a tight schedule. Reluctantly I pushed myself even harder with the running until I had left the village and made the steep descent from the Mendips until I reached Wells.

The whole of my body now felt painfully tired from the hard 30-mile push, which incorporated as many hills as possible, with the least amount of food and drink having been consumed.

At Wells I had two support runners join me for the final section, which would take me over a steady seven mile incline all the way to Shepton Mallet before finishing in the village of Chelynch.

The first thing that the two new runners asked me was if I was okay, as I looked awful. I then tried to convince them about what I was aiming to achieve as we ran out of Wells and into the narrow streets of neighbouring villages.

The cold night sky quickly surrounded us in darkness, as we ran across sodden, muddy fields which unmercifully taunted us. The worst was when we unexpectedly trod in a deep cow rut, resulting in a disgusting plume of sludge instantly splashing up over the front of us.

With only three-and-a-half miles remaining, I was determined not to stop or take any more refreshments. Several times my support runners would ask me if I was alright, to which I would reassure them I was, even though I couldn't even manage to hold a reasonable conversation!

With each landmark, I knew we were nearly finished and that

this run through sodden fields on a freezing winter's evening would soon be over.

Just ahead of me appeared the welcoming lights of the Poachers Pocket pub in Chelynch.

I had made this difficult run despite minimal food and rest, but now knew what the warning signs were for any longer runs in the future. Finding out how I felt while under these conditions proved so important, as I now knew my boundaries.

Quickly changing out of my wet running gear into dry clothes I tucked into the biggest steak on the menu. It was worth every minute of what I had put myself through. Now it was time to sit back and relax for a short while before returning back to the drawing board and planning my next adventure!

***

With all the new activities going on in my life, the months passed by as though they were only weeks. With all my training sessions in the evenings and on weekends, events that had been planned months ahead arrived so quickly. It felt as though I was going straight from one big run into another, with very little rest.

The more I learnt from my running experiences, the more I wanted to share with others. Instead of taking part in half marathon and marathon races to gain a new personal best, I now found more pleasure helping pace others that I had helped to train. I enjoyed seeing them cross the finish line in a time that they wouldn't have thought possible beforehand.

In between all my longer runs, which I had increased from one-a-year to three-a-year, I still felt the familiar signs of the seizures returning. They would mostly happen during the night after resting in the same position for more than a few hours. Luckily I could still remove the pain by exercising, which would give me back my freedom. However, if I were to travel or sit operating site machinery for several hours, I would experience difficulty in walking or stepping down from the operating plant.

I always thought how lucky I was to still be able to compete with some of the best runners while facing all these demons, even though most people around me would casually reassure me that every event I entered would be an easy one to complete because of my running success to date. Little did they know how hard a personal battle each one had become.

It was always a challenge breaking through the first 18-mile barrier on each event. I would try and ignore the mileage at every start, and just reward myself by passing various landmarks. I also made sure that I had support runners to distract me with conversation.

There would be days, after a really bad night of seizures and total lack of sleep, that I wouldn't have any interest in running. But to everyone around me this would be hidden by a mask of smiles, as I didn't want to let anyone down with my own misfortunes.

After many hospital appointments and check-ups throughout the years to find a solution for the seizures, but to no avail, I decided that the only cure for me was to continue with the running. I certainly didn't want to go back on any strong medication by any means, that would only be a very last resort.

Only a month after my last 100-mile run in November, I could feel the seizures returning once more and knew I would have to try and organise another long run before the end of the year.

For hours on end I studied the road atlas again, along with OS maps, in the hope of putting together another ultra-event. The main problem I faced was that it had to be reasonably local so that I could co-ordinate it around work without having to use all my holiday. Also, there would be long stretches on my own which meant that I had to carry and replace vital food supplies somewhere on route.

Running for days on end also meant the route had to be interesting so that it provided a distraction from the duration and mileage.

Eventually, I devised a run which would take me from where I live in Westfield all the way into Bath, Bristol, Chew Valley, the length of the Mendip Hills and finally back to Westfield, covering 74 miles a day.

The plan would be for me to quickly shower and change each day while passing my home and, if possible, snatch a few hours of sleep before setting off to run the same circuit again.

I would be passing through towns and country pubs that at certain times I knew would be open, enabling me to get a hot meal when needed.

With a new sense of excitement, I couldn't wait to try out this new circuit to see what it had in store for me. The last thing that I wanted to do was run the same old circuit again that I had been using for the previous three years. I now needed something fresh to explore to keep my momentum on a high. So I wasted no more time and put together a brand-new timetable for the 74-mile route.

Saturday 3rd December, 2011

At 4am I was woken by the sound of my alarm clock dancing across the top of my bedside table. It seemed to purposely torment me by vibrating just out of arm's reach, so that I had to make a conscious effort to catch it!

Still half asleep I thought I could hear the sound of a heavy rain storm, so reluctantly I peered out of the bedroom window to investigate. Sure enough, I could see the torrential rain as it fell, sweeping along in waves highlighted by the bright overhead streetlamps.

Looking across to Paddo, I nearly surrendered to the thought of climbing back into a warm cosy bed. All my kit had been packed the previous evening, so all that was needed now was a good bowl of warm porridge to set me up for the day.

With the rain now turning into a misty drizzle, I left home at

5am and ran the ten miles into Bath where the first signs of daybreak began to appear.

Supporting a fresh cup of coffee, I reflected on past memories of finishing in front of the Abbey before continuing my way around the other magnificent landmarks of Bath. The Circus, Royal Crescent and Victoria Park were great distractions from the mileage as I made my way through the city. By 10am I was sitting in a cosy café in Keynsham enjoying a bacon roll along with another fresh brew of coffee, thoroughly enjoying the new route and all it had to offer!

As I entered Bristol, I found the usual traffic chaos, but was rewarded by passing the magnificent Bristol Cathedral and Will's Memorial Building at the top of Park Street before crossing Brunel's Suspension Bridge. It was here that the sun managed to break through all the dark clouds and cast her golden spell down onto the picturesque Avon Gorge below.

Running up to Bedminster Down after passing by the football stadium, I managed to find a convenient snack van selling bacon rolls and coffee. Briefly while indulging in my picnic, I enjoyed the view back over Bristol with the Suspension Bridge now standing some four miles in the distance.

The long unforgiving hill of Dundry was a real challenge for my legs at the half-way point of my route. People often ask why I add such huge hills to my circuits; the reason is that I find they disperse a lot of the lactic acid that accumulates in the muscles compared to running a flat route. By adding the steep ascents I use my arms, shoulders and back a lot more in order to power up them and always feel a lot better afterwards.

After leaving Dundry it was a deep descent through narrow country lanes before arriving in the quiet village of Winford. I found that descending steep inclines was just as painful, if not moreso, than ascending. To overcome this I had learnt to lean backwards and run with much shorter footsteps to reduce the impact on my knees and hips.

Just as I entered Winford, I had a phone call from Bob who met me minutes later at the far end of the village. It felt good to have company and a great distraction from the tiredness that had started to niggle away at me.

I had really enjoyed the route so far, covering fresh trails and sights that I would never have seen otherwise.

I was now only halfway, and it had been a hard 38-mile route, running on my own carrying all my supplies. It was now 4pm and the sun had given in to the advancing darkness as my route undulated across Chew Valley.

The silvery moon was reflected on the still surface of Chew Valley Lake. Apart from the occasional passing car or ducks, there was total silence in this magical landscape. This is what makes running overnight so special. I forget all the negative aspects and embrace all the sights around me.

After another steep climb to the top of the Mendip Hills via East Harptree, our reward was to arrive at the Castle of Comfort pub for a cool pint of Guinness and meet up with more support runners.

After a quick change into a running jacket and leggings to keep out the bitter cold, we were soon running again, through the dark lanes of the Mendips. After passing several villages including Priddy and Wookey Hole, we arrived in Wells where the weather decided to turn into a torrential downpour, resulting in torrents of water gushing down the narrow high street.

I was now 60 miles into the run with only 13 miles remaining. I had only another half marathon distance left to travel and would soon be back in the comfort of my own home.

After thanking everyone for supporting me, I left the dry sanctuary of Poet's Corner in the market square in Wells and ventured out into the pouring rain to complete the run.

Eight miles further on, the rain suddenly stopped and with a parting of the clouds the moon appeared. Within minutes the whole of the landscape around me had totally changed. Glancing across sodden fields back towards Shepton Mallet from the top of Bodden Cross, I could see the magnificent Charlton Viaduct, its 27 huge stone arches now reflecting the moons silver light.

As the last miles of country lanes disappeared behind me, the only sound that could be heard was of my feet splashing through water on the flooded tarmac below.

At midnight, just as the moon had finished guiding me home, it disappeared once more into the embrace of the immense storm clouds.

In 19 hours, I had completed the entire 74-mile circuit, two hours ahead of my planned schedule. I had found the new route to be both interesting and reasonably comfortable (as any route of that distance could be), and would be available for me to use for future events.

Sitting in the comfort of my old armchair, surrounded by my dogs – who were all fighting to climb onto my lap at the same time – I felt relieved that I had completed the circuit. Now it was time to relax for a while and forget about chasing time schedules. Deep down inside I knew I had a fresh challenge awaiting me, but that would have to wait a while until I had caught up with several urgent jobs that needed my attention around the cottage.

GALE FORCE CHALLENGE

Just days after finishing the 74-mile circuit, I had an email from the Olympic Relay team to inform me that, unfortunately, I hadn't had my first nomination accepted. I felt an immediate sense of disappointment. Although I still held onto the happy memories of my first correspondence with the team back in August, I deliberately kept my hopes low throughout the following months.

Then, day after day, I received a similar email informing me that yet another two nominations had been refused. I tried my best to look at the positive side of things by remembering that it was amazing to have been selected for a nomination in the first place, but that did little to help the feeling of disappointment I still carried.

Finally, on a Friday evening after returning home from work, I switched on my laptop to see that I had been contacted again regarding my fourth and final nomination result. Walking away from the laptop, I was too nervous to open the message because I didn't want my last hope to be shattered. Instead I carried on cooking my tea before returning back to the dining room some 45 minutes later.

Standing over the laptop, I reluctantly opened the email and again walked away to my little sanctuary of not knowing the outcome! Shaking through sheer nervousness, I returned to read the email congratulating me on a conditional offer to be a London 2012 Olympic Torchbearer! I stood on the same spot and read the email another four times before I could believe it.

I immediately printed off the message, just to see it written on paper, so it felt even more real and I could actually hold it in my hands. I now had to fill in all the relevant forms for security checks and would have confirmation by March 2012.

The thought of having the honour to be accepted to carry the Olympic Torch in an area close to where I lived was indescribable. Time and time again I would wake up in the night and ponder for a while if I had actually dreamt the whole thing.

I wasn't allowed to release any information to anyone until March 2012 regarding the relay, so until then I decided to keep the whole situation a secret in order not to jeopardise my chances.

With all the excitement regarding the 2012 Olympic games, I desperately wanted to put another run together and set myself a new long-distance record.

I had previously reached 300 miles, but now I wanted to show the world what could be achieved if you remain positive against all the odds. The next break that I could take from work would be the week over Christmas.

Looking back at the 74-mile circuit I had completed at the beginning of December, I had finished feeling reasonably comfortable. I then wondered if I could run the same circuit continuously over a period of five days!

The new run would take me 70 miles further than I had ever ran before, and would be reasonably local if anyone wished to join me. This would also take me very close to the world record, held at that time by an American athlete who ran 410 miles over a seven-day period!

For hours on end I studied all my local maps looking for alternative routes and finally decided that I would run my new 74-mile circuit. Instead of running it all anti-clockwise for the whole duration, I would alternate the route from day to day, just to make it less monotonous.

Having broken up from work on 23rd December for the Christmas break, I had everything in place in preparation for my longest run. Food supplies had been prepared to cover each day, press statements had been released, and news of my event was now appearing in all the local papers along with my radio interviews to raise awareness for the CHSW charity. I also released a timetable to all the local running clubs to see if anyone would like to join me at any stage of the event.

370-mile run, 26th-31st December, 2011

On a cold, damp Boxing Day morning I left home carrying all my essential supplies for the start of my five-day journey.

It was 8am and the roads were really quiet as everyone seemed to be making the most of their time-off over the festive period.

As always the first few miles of my run seemed particularly challenging with the apprehension of what I was about to take on. On the long runs I had to remain absolutely positive at all times, no matter what odds were stacked against me. Subconsciously there were flashes of negativity telling me that although the run into Bath had gone well and all those hills were now behind me, I still had another 360 miles to run over the same circuit, continuously for the next four days!

For miles I would argue with my imaginary demon on one shoulder, pouring out negativity, then hang on to the positive reassurance from my guardian angel on the other.

After the first day I managed to quickly change, shower and snatch an hour's sleep before departing for the next day's run. This time I decided to run the 74-mile circuit clockwise to try and break up the monotony. At first this seemed to work but as the day progressed it just didn't feel comfortable. For hours on end I fought with myself, trying to feel positive about running the circuit back to front, but it felt like a real struggle. I never felt so relieved to descend the final hill into Westfield during the early hours of Wednesday morning!

The second day had put me an hour behind schedule, which meant that I could only afford to have half-an-hour's sleep before setting off on the third day's run.

Running up and out of the hills surrounding Westfield, I could now feel my body starting to protest over what I was putting it through. I could have so easily stayed at home and had just another hour of sleep.

Through all the aches and pains, and a deep sense of tiredness, I continually reminded myself that I was still on target on my schedule. This is so important because once you know that you are behind it can pose a huge negative outlook and use up so much precious mental energy.

Continuously, support runners would phone me to see where I was on my schedule and then surprise me by turning up in the least expected of places at all hours. This helped me immensely to stay motivated and focused on my target.

The weather up until now had been reasonably good, but on the third evening everything was about to change for the worse.

At 11:30pm, just as I began to enter the village of Priddy, high on top of the Mendip Hills, it began to rain. What started as a gentle storm soon developed into a force seven gale, making running head-long into the torrential rain almost impossible. Several times I tried to tighten my waterproof jacket to stop the storm from seeping through, but to no avail. Water just streamed down inside from the strength of the wind, and in no time I was soaking wet from head to foot.

It was a great relief when I was joined by Pat and Chris who had brought out hot drinks and snacks for me to indulge in whenever we could find somewhere slightly sheltered to stop. Several times throughout the night I would quickly snatch a drink along with a snack in order to keep up sufficient energy levels. This was particularly needed with the cold chill of the storm biting into your core within minutes.

Rewarding myself by passing familiar landmarks I continued on through the bitter night to safely arrive in Westfield, again an hour short of my scheduled time.

The warmth of a hot shower felt really good, as it drove the chill from my bones, along with most of the aches and pains that had accumulated over the last three days.

I could only have half-an-hour's sleep before setting back out on the fourth day's run. I knew that this would be the toughest day. I was just over the halfway mark and still had two complete days of running to achieve. But there was no way I could keep thinking this way otherwise it would destroy all my drive.

Various radio stations rang me for an update on my progress which gave me a great boost of confidence, especially when people recognised me while out on the circuit. Others would get familiar seeing me pass the same location each day especially while on their way to work or on building sites. Often people would shout out "keep going, you can do it" or "how much further to go now?"

Halfway through the fourth day my body seemed to almost give up fighting. Up until then it had constantly bombarded me with every ache and pain possible, along with the huge mental battle. Now, I suddenly felt as though all the aches and pains had almost gone. Perhaps I had become so used to them that they had become acceptable!

The rain continued to fall but without the strong winds of the previous day. Lorries would constantly splash dirty water up over the pavements as they drove by, leaving me soaked to the skin. Whenever the storm clouds parted and the sun briefly returned, I would dry out and then feel the dirty black dust left behind which covered my exposed legs and arms.

Several teams of runners from different clubs came out to join me through the toughest of times, which I found to be mainly around 3pm going into the early stages of the night. While running through the darkness of night, I found that the time passed quickly. Whether it is because you can't see too far into the distance or the height of the hills that you have to pass over – I don't know – probably in my case it's because I needed to be at a particular location much earlier and needed to pick the pace up.

The final ten miles of hilly countryside proved very demanding at the end of the fourth day, and by the time I got home I had to deal with several large blisters on each of my feet that had accumulated through running in wet socks.

After a quick hot shower and patching up my feet – which now resembled something out of a horror film – I was leaving Westfield devoid of sleep for the fifth and final day. I tried to reassure my poor legs that this would be the last time they would have to climb all those hills into Bath again – for at least a few months!

Thankfully Richard and Vicky, my neighbours, were taking my dogs out several times a day and were a great help in organising my home life, making this challenge possible.

Several cars blew their horns and familiar faces shouted words of encouragement as I made my way for the final time through the busy streets of Bath and Bristol. At last the weather improved and I could keep my poor feet dry.

Waves of sudden tiredness would sweep over me and almost force me to stop. After several cups of coffee from cafés while running through Bristol it seemed to briefly pass. But I found myself, when trying to run in a straight line along a narrow footpath on Clifton Down, veering off sideways as if I had too much to drink in the local pub! The harder I tried to concentrate on running in a straight line, the worse it got.

I decided that I desperately needed a quick power nap and thankfully found a park bench to crash out on. Leaning back across the bench I didn't even find the time to release my backpack before nodding off into a really deep sleep. I woke up 20 minutes later staring up at my flag fluttering away from above of my backpack. Unclutching the rolled up laminated schedule from my cold hands, I was now 20 minutes behind time.

Springing to my feet, I now felt a lot better and thought that I had learnt a valuable lesson in which to stop if I ever felt that tired again. I had lost a lot of ground trying to force myself on and was now travelling two, if not three times faster than before. Continuing at a good pace I soon made up for the time I had lost earlier.

The huge climb over Dundry and the Mendip Hills was relentless but offered breathtaking views as ever. Chris and Pat re-joined me and spoilt me as usual with plenty of refreshments to keep me going through the night. While I had the chance, I also managed to have a quick ten minute power nap in the front seat of Chris's car before it got later into the evening, when sleep deprivation was sure to have set in.

As the sun rose to bring daylight into the new day, I had a heart-warming surprise waiting for me as I ran into the village of Chelynch. Patiently waiting for me was a whole group of runners from Wells, MH4 and Somer Athletic club to guide me through the final eight miles of hills to the finish line.

Looking around I could see little Paddo with Rich and Vicky, straining away on his lead to try and reach me. With Paddo now in my arms I thanked everyone for all their amazing support and for coming out so early to join me. With an incredible team spirit, I was guided over the last of the hills to finish with a huge reception at the Miner's Wheel monument in Radstock.

It had been a brutal five days out on the road with only four hours sleep, an estimated 40,000 calories burnt, covering 14 marathons back to back, achieving my own personal record of running 370 continuous miles. The publicity that this run had attracted was also immense and helped the CHSW charity a great deal with funding and awareness.

I was now only 40 miles short of achieving the Guinness world record, which then stood at 408.04 miles in seven days, by Mike Sheehy in San Diego. Could it be done? How could I extend my run for another two days, knowing how much it hurt, behind all the hidden smiles that I portrayed to everyone?

As it was now New Year's Eve, I arranged to meet a lot of the support runners later that evening in the local pub, where we could celebrate and discuss what adventures the year 2012 might bring us all.

As everyone counted down to celebrate the New Year, I stood alone for a short while. I was a million miles away, lost deep in thoughts about what my cousins Phil and Steve would have to say. I really missed their company and banter. Then suddenly I was back into full celebration, having never felt so excited as to what possibilities the year ahead might bring. But I still had to wait a couple of long months until I would receive final conformation about carrying the Olympic Torch.

***

My priority now became getting all the preparations in place for my next big run in which I would try to break the world record.

I decided that I would start the event on Tuesday 1st May and finish the following Bank Holiday Monday.

The aim of the run was to raise as much awareness as possible for the CHSW charity, and to show others that sometimes impossible dreams can become a reality if you truly believe in what you set out to achieve. I was also hoping to attract as much attention as I could to our community at Westfield, and the schools that I had visited.

Had I not had radiotherapy back in 2004 then none of my running adventures and goals would ever have been achieved. Most likely I would be in the same routine of work and paying the bills. I would have been totally oblivious to the fact that I was able to achieve any one of the amazing goals I had achieved over the last eight years.

This run wouldn't rely on huge sponsorship from famous brands or top sports coaches, it would be attempted by a solo person who was still working 60 manual hours a week, supported by a handful of people who truly believed that I would be strong enough to see this event through to the end. Whether I broke the world record or not made no difference. I would at least have a good attempt at it and give everything I could purely by using the spirit of all the good friends around me.

A sense of pure excitement would fill my body every time I paused to consider the run. My poor old heart rate would increase as adrenalin raced through my body. All I could concentrate on now was breaking the world record.

In the back of my mind I carried so many nagging thoughts that would continuously surface, as I questioned my ability to organise and complete this scale of event. During the night I would wake up with vivid memories of the previous five-day run, and how it had punished me. But what I liked most about these events was the fun that I had running with great company. I've heard just about every subject of conversation available. It's surprising what words you hear from the front of the pack, especially when climbing those steep hills!

When you are physically exhausted the simplest of things can sometimes make or break you. I can remember on one event overhearing a conversation behind me, someone saying that they would have to speed up the pace in order to get back for a party later that evening. This left me feeling really despondent as to why I was behind schedule, and my pace became even slower with all my negative thoughts. On other occasions, if I had a radio interview or someone on the road recognised me and gave me encouragement, I would suddenly increase my pace as if I had been refuelled, and my support team would have to slow me down!

After many meetings with CHSW and attending press and radio interviews, the months of January and February suddenly disappeared. Before I knew it, it was March, and I had the incredible confirmation that I was going to be part of the London 2012 team carrying the Olympic torch in Frome on 22nd May.

Shaking with disbelief, I immediately printed the confirmation email, as though it might disappear, then printed it off again. One copy I kept on the dining room table, and the other I filed away safely!

Earlier that year I had the pleasure of meeting British athlete Steve Cram, a hero of mine who was the first man to run 1500m in under three minutes, 30 seconds. He won a gold medal at the world championships in Helsinki and silver at the Olympic games in 1984. His words of encouragement were a great inspiration to me and something that I never forgot every time I got pre-race nerves.

April was a beautiful month with plenty of sunshine to introduce the warmth and colours of spring; the long, dark and wet days of winter now seemed a distant memory.

Each morning I would wake up to the enormity of what lay ahead of me. But any doubts would be cast aside and overidden by messages of support from people I had never met. It felt as though they were long-term friends offering such kindness and reassurance.

With all the plans for the latest challenge now firmly in place, I had a brilliant support crew who I could trust 100% and every eventuality that I could think of was covered. I booked my time off from work, and with only one week to go a fresh change of kit was laid out at home for each consecutive day, along with my food and a gas stove.

The night before the run I double checked that everything was in order. I laminated each days' schedule for me to carry at all times, along with another that would stay with the recording ledger for each support crew to fill in times, location and mileage each day.

It was a complete waste of time even attempting to go to bed that evening, as my pulse was racing, and schedules were going through my mind as well as an endless checklist. I just wanted to be out there on the run now and put all my nervous energy into some useful mileage!

HOW THE WEEK RAN AWAY

On Tuesday 1st May at 6am I switched on the radio only to hear on the local news the announcement that I would be starting my event later that morning. It felt really good to hear this but at the same time filled me with apprehension because the whole world knew what was expected of me. Just after the news, an amber flood warning was issued for the days ahead, which immediately made my heart sink. April had been such a good month, perfect for running with plenty of sunshine in the day and clear cold evenings.

I began to curse myself as I cautiously looked out of the window and watched the torrential rain sweeping past. Thinking positively, I still had another two hours to go until I started. Perhaps by then there would be a break in the weather and the worst of the storm might have passed. Nervously I made a huge bowl of porridge and another pot of tea to fuel me for the run.

At 7:45am Bob arrived, cursing the weather, along with Kevin and Martyn, who were my support drivers for the day. After loading the supplies and kit, it was time for me to start the long week ahead.

The wind and rain showed no mercy. The road outside my house had now flooded where the drains could no longer cope with the sheer volume of water.

Marg, my neighbour, braved the storm to come out and wish me good luck, clutching her umbrella as tight as she could to shelter from all the rain.

At exactly 8am both Bob and myself started the run, closely followed by the support vehicle. The busy morning traffic splashed the pavements as they drove through all the accumulating flood water.

Our bare legs were now covered in muddy grime and our trainers were completely saturated within the first 100 metres of what would be an incredibly long run.

Drivers would beep their horns and people shouted words of encouragement as they passed, which helped enormously. My Union Jack flag was now stuck sodden against the small standard that rose from the top of my backpack.

As we climbed the first ten miles of unforgiving hills into Bath, we encountered several manhole covers that had lifted under the sheer enormity of the flood water. We now faced exposed fountains of water on the roads and pavements.

The weather showed no sign of ceasing as we battled against the odds. Occasionally I would look over at Bob who would shake his head at me and tell me what a bloody idiot I was, which would make me burst out laughing and raise my spirits.

Outside the Royal Crescent in Bath, I was greeted by Kevin, who quickly ran over with a much-appreciated cup of hot coffee. Luckily the storm clouds briefly parted and I managed a quick respite from the rain. Miles away deep in thought, I suddenly became aware that I was surrounded by a group of tourists who had just got off a tour bus. They had been attracted to my flag and wondered what the occasion was. After a quick photo and wishing me good luck with my run, I was soon making my way towards Bristol and even more torrential rain!

Thanking Bob for joining me under such dismal conditions, I continued my way through the city centre and on to the magnificent views out over the Clifton Suspension Bridge. Again, there was a very brief spell of fine weather where I could feel the warmth of the sun's rays on my cold legs, but that was to be disappointingly short lived as the relentless rain returned. On several occasions I changed my wet socks, but this proved to be a complete waste of time as most of the country lanes were now deep in flood water. The fields surrounding Chew Valley overflowed with torrents of water, and even the ford in Chew Stoke was impassable due to the rise in the river level, forcing us to change our route at the last minute.

Soon, night time fell as I approached the Mendip Hills; the rain had now stopped and been replaced by a damp misty air. I felt so relieved to be running without a waterproof jacket for the first time that day.

I was nearly an hour-and-a-half ahead of schedule as Martyn and Kevin finished their support shift at 10:30pm and were replaced by Viv in the village of Wookey Hole. I felt reasonably comfortable despite the atrocious weather, apart from my feet which had started to break down after being constantly wet all day.

My regular intake of foods had worked well so far, along with a constant supply of hot drinks. Occasionaly support runners would unexpectedly turn up and join me, which provided great company while at other times I would be on my own just with the support vehicle. This balanced out nicely, as I would lose myself in what I would describe as recovery running. This form of recovery running was when I would almost completely shut down my body from the outside world. I would be fully aware of everything going on around me, especially traffic, undulating roads and various surfaces, but at the same time, I could rest from conversation and thinking.

I would give Viv in the support car a huge thumbs up signal if I didn't want to stop, or a hand to mouth gesture if I needed to stop for a quick drink or snack at the next marked location on the schedule.

At 5am, I arrived back at home an hour-and-a-half ahead of schedule, after covering the first circuit of 74 miles virtually non-stop. I felt so pleased with the first day's result and thanked Viv for all his support as he dropped off all the supplies ready for the next vehicle to be loaded.

Quickly I got showered and changed, sorted out more food and added several more pairs of socks into my kit bag for the day ahead. After eating a large bowl of porridge and snatching 30 minutes sleep in the comfort of my armchair, I was helping to load the support car, before setting off again at 7:30am.

It was difficult running out of Westfield that morning. My mind was willing and full of enthusiasm but my body didn't want to respond in the same way. My feet started to show the first signs of deterioration as they quickly got wet again from flooded pavements and the constant spray from passing traffic. Again the weather proved atrocious with heavy downpours of rain and only the slightest glimpse of sunshine.

After the first ten miles I changed my sodden socks for some fresh ones, but each time I stopped it proved difficult to start running again. This wasn't a good sign, especially as I had only just started my second day and had another five to follow.

While running through the town of Keynsham, I was stopped by a group of pensioners who had waited for me to give a donation, after seeing me on the local news. To me this is what my runs are all about, meeting people and having a quick chat after they had made the kind effort to come out and see me. Feeling much more confident and rejuvenated with enthusiasm, I soon found myself running through the steep streets of Bristol to arrive at the suspension bridge once more.

Unknown to me, waiting at the bridge were members of the CHSW care team, along with several children from the local hospice, all sporting gorgeous smiles and cheers of encouragement.

This was a massive boost to my morale. Despite the weather they had still come out to give their support. Immediately I forgot all about my problems and all my other aches and pains. All the smiles and support were priceless and filled me with a new strength. For a while I stood and talked to the children and their care staff, who had formed a small circle around me. Some were in their wheel chairs while others bounced excitedly on their toes holding onto staff members.

After giving a huge cheer, everyone followed me slowly across Clifton Suspension Bridge in formation. Halfway across the bridge I heard a young girl shout "run, run, as fast as you can, you can't catch me, I'm the gingerbread man", which brought a smile to everyone and small tears to my face. That one sentence from the little girl really drove home to me why I had taken on this massive challenge. It was to represent them and hopefully raise a lot of vital funding to help their families.

Looking back over my shoulder I gave one last cheer and a huge wave. Leaving all the tiny voices behind me, I descended into the Avon Gorge below, carrying memories that will stay with me forever.

Running through unforgiving storms and torrents of rain, I suddenly found that I had lost the hour-and-a-half that I had gained on the first day. I was now back on my original schedule with no time to spare. It was up to me to work even harder again to try and gain some spare time, in case of any unforseen eventualities.

Smitham's Hill is an unforgiving climb that stretches for two-and-a-half miles until you reach the welcome sight of the Castle of Comfort pub at the top. On reaching the hill I started to feel really tired as the first signs of sleep deprivation were beginning to invade. Looking ahead I could just make out, through the narrow beam of light from my headtorch, a small group of support runners, patiently waiting in the darkness ahead. This quickly brought me back to my senses, giving me a much needed burst of energy for the long climb before me.

Where there had been so much rain, parts of the roadside had been washed away and the pub at the bottom of the hill was flooded.

In the steeper parts of the climb I had to give my poor legs some help by pushing down firmly on top of my knees to keep the momentum going. This, along with good conversation and a lot of humour from the other runners, soon powered me to the top of the hill and the welcome sight of the pub.

While at the pub I had a pint of Guinness, purely for medicinal purposes, and a large plate of chips, which would be sufficient to see me into the early hours of the following morning. In total I had a break of just 30 minutes before I continued my way across the dark, bleak Mendip Hills.

Getting started again after the break was hard work until I could release all the lactic acid from my legs. With this in mind I decided to skip the next planned break and convinced myself that I was now fully fuelled for the next 25 miles until I reached home again. This way I would hopefully gain some time. All I had to do was dismiss the pain I was now experiencing from my sodden trainers!

All through the night the rain kept coming, sweeping across in front of me, obscuring the view of the road ahead as it appeared as one large white blanket in the beam of my headtorch. Suddenly, in the darkness, my feet would disappear into a large muddy puddle that completely covered the width of the narrow road. The freezing cold water brought instant relief to my hot feet for a moment, until I could feel my raw exposed skin sliding against my trainers again.

The way that I dealt with pain was to try not to concentrate on what was hurting, but instead to focus on all the good things that I would be encountering later on in my run.

At midnight we swapped support vehicles and I was still just ahead of schedule which made me feel very happy. I knew I needed to keep ahead at all costs.

Suddenly, at 3am while making a steep climb over a mile-long hill at Bodden, I felt really exhausted. I knew I had to give in and take a quick power nap, but really didn't want to lose any of the time I had gained.

The more I fought the tiredness, the worse I felt. I found myself running sideways instead of straight and on several occasions bumped into the side of fellow runners. It must have been less than a minute after sitting in the front seat of the support car that I instantly fell asleep. After just ten minutes I woke, still clutching the schedule in my hand and continued my run. Quickly noticing that I had no time to spare regarding the schedule, I made every effort to increase my pace until I reached the safety of home at 6am. I always found it amazing that after just ten minutes of deep sleep the body and mind can feel so refreshed.

Rushing into home for a quick, painful, hot shower, I couldn't believe how much of my kit had caused friction burns to my body after two days of running in the rain.

Feeling really tired I began to question myself if it was worth all I was putting my body through. After contemplating all my positive memories I soon refocused, and realised that my hour at home was nearly up. The next support car had already arrived!

I smeared my sore feet with antiseptic cream while finishing off my breakfast, as my support crew loaded their car with my kit.

Devoid of any sleep and with the rain still pouring down, the thought of running through another day of bad weather really didn't appeal to me.

But through all the tiredness and self-doubt, I got changed, had another cup of hot tea, then locked the front door before leaving the comfort of home to run another 74-mile circuit. The difference this time was that I was now one hour and 20 minutes behind schedule!

I started off running down the pavements of Westfield in a very awkward manner; every step that I took was so painful, even though my feet were now covered in a patchwork of plasters. Several runners had braved the weather to come along to the start and support me when most needed. One runner even held an umbrella over me as we ran, sheltering me from the storm, while others provided greatly appreciated moral support.

Again, exposed manhole covers sprayed storm water up to a foot high as the pressure hurled heavy cast iron lids to one side.

We all shared what we called 'umbrella shifts' to try and shelter from both the strong winds and heavy rain, but with all the surface spray coming from the passing traffic it made very little difference.

I was so glad to reach the city of Bath and be clear of all the main roads and traffic, where I could be partially sheltered from the storm. The huge buildings and parks provided a much welcome sanctuary of peace and quiet.

Reaching the far end of one of the parks, I could see the support crew surrounding the little gas stove to shelter it from the wind and keep them warm. On approaching I could see my breath as it hit the cold air around me. I gratefully warmed my hands around a cup of hot soup and couldn't help but wonder what had happened to all the fine weather that we had back in April.

Despite all the atrocious weather, painful feet and being behind schedule, I was so lucky to have the best support crew anyone could ever wish for, which kept me positive and focused on what we were hoping to achieve.

Every day I would have regular radio and TV interviews as people wanted to know how things were progressing. People going to work or taking their children to school would look out for us and shout words of encouragement when least expected.

While making my way into Bristol I briefly stopped to meet my Aunt. She had brought a hot flask of my favourite chicken soup along with a delicious homemade bread pudding. This tasted like pure heaven and I was soon full of the best food in the world. It was so good to see her and it made me realise how much she cared about me.

When I told her that my legs were really sore, she quickly gave them a much needed massage. Feeling half asleep while still standing, this caught me by surprise and I ended up spilling soup over her back, much to the horror of those watching.

After all the food intake, I felt really tired and took a ten-minute power nap in the front seat of the support car. While I slept, the crew disappeared into the local burger bar to refuel.

Back out running, I received a phone call from Radio Bristol inviting us to come into their studio for a live interview. This was an opportunity I certainly couldn't turn down, to raise awareness for the CHSW charity. So, we ran up to their studio and went out live on air for about ten minutes. I always enjoyed the interviews because they were a lot of fun and full of good humour.

On reaching the suspension bridge again, I found that the weather was taking a huge toll, both physically and mentally, and I was now three-and-a-half hours behind schedule.

At the beginning of the run I had estimated that I could run between 440–450 miles over the seven days. But now I knew that wasn't going to happen; I just needed to focus on breaking the 408.04 miles in seven days world record.

After crossing the bridge, the sun broke through a gap in the storm clouds, raising the temperature almost immediately. Slowly but surely the clouds started to disperse, surrounding us in constant sunshine. For the first time in 55 hours I could now comfortably run without wearing a jacket. I now had the bright sunshine reflecting off the flooded road surface and it felt so good to be running in the warm sunshine.

Approaching the bottom of Dundry Hill I could see Bob and Margaret eagerly awaiting my arrival with fresh snacks and a steaming mug of coffee. Margaret commented on how sunburnt I was around my face. It didn't feel warm and I just put it down to the sudden change in weather conditions. A few minutes later Margaret was kindly applying sun cream to my burnt face. Immediately I felt so relaxed and tired that without warning I fell asleep stood upright, with her propping me up to stop me from toppling over.

It wasn't until my phone rang a few minutes later that I woke up in a state of startlement to find everyone smiling at the fact that I could sleep while standing up!

For the first time on the event, I managed to run through the entire evening without it pouring down with rain. It made everything so much easier and enjoyable.

Even though I found it easier to run through the early hours of Thursday morning, sleep deprivation was starting to set in and do its best to take over my mind and body. To combat the situation, I would snatch ten-minute power naps in the front seat of the support vehicle.

Approaching Wells at 6:25am, having so far covered 205 miles, I was met by a fellow runner, Jayne, who informed me that she had a cooked breakfast waiting for us all. With her house only minutes away, I decided to take my scheduled break earlier than originally planned.

The breakfast was amazing – a full English with several mugs of tea. While eating, my poor feet were also receiving some much needed attention. I felt much like a racing car that had just pulled into the pits and received major attention before quickly going back out onto the track again.

I couldn't believe how good everyone was in supporting and believing in me. Each day, whatever the hour or weather condition, I would find Roger and Lee-Anne quietly waiting for me by the small clock tower at the bottom of East Harptree hill. They would gently run with me for two-and-a-half miles to the top of the Mendip Hills, to make sure that I accomplished one of the hardest and most demanding hills on the circuit.

Another example were my cousin's little ones, Jess and Ryan, who, after attending Priddy Primary School, would get their mother to find me so that they could join in and run at least three to five miles with me each day, depending on conditions and the weather.

It was through so many acts of kindness like these – too many to mention – that I believed in what I set out to achieve.

I finally finished the third circuit at 11:35am on Friday morning, and I staggered into home, leaving my bedraggled backpack in the middle of the living room along with a trail of clothes that led to the bathroom.

I couldn't wait to have a much needed soak under a really hot shower. I must have leant against the wall for a good 20 minutes before deciding that I needed to get my act together and head out and do the same thing all over again.

Subconsciously, I hid the fact that I still had to do the whole thing all over again for another three days, so I just focused on completing another 74-mile circuit as though it was the final one.

Just over an hour after arriving back at home, I was patched up and ready to face another day of running. It was hard leaving the comforts of home. I often wondered if it would have been easier to have run in unfamiliar surroundings, but I loved the daily encouragement from everyone looking out for me and wanting to be part of the event.

Reflecting on how bad a condition my feet were in, I really didn't think I could have continued with the run if it hadn't stopped raining. As long as I dodged the huge puddles that still lay in the country lanes my feet would remain dry.

I was now running solo on autopilot, in a completely relaxed mode where I could save a lot of energy. I didn't have to engage in conversation, and the only things that I had to concentrate on were maintaining my pace and being aware of pedestrians and traffic. When other support runners joined me, I was always grateful for their company and enjoyed their distracting conversations – so I had the best of both worlds.

Today, my running seemed to flow so much easier. The weather conditions were far better and my body seemed to let go of any restrictions as everything felt far less demanding.

On reaching Clifton Suspension Bridge at 10:52pm, the structure looked amazing at night, illuminated by hundreds of bulbs across its entire span.

While I was quietly mesmerised by the view of Bristol, lit up for miles before me, I suddenly heard a couple of young voices behind me that I instantly recognised. It was little Jess and Ryan who had come out to find me. Thoughts came flooding back of when the children and support team from CHSW had run with me earlier in the week. This time I could do the same, but with my little Godson and his sister.

By 1am I had conquered Dundry Hill once more. From the top

I could see the far away lights of the suspension bridge, while in the opposite direction there was the distant glow of red from the city of Wells illuminating the night sky, some 22 miles ahead of us.

Passing through the stillness of Priddy village at 6am, the sun began to rise into a new day, revealing incredible views out over the Somerset Levels. Hidden treasures like the famous Glastonbury Tor revealed themselves from the clenches of a fine mist that spread below us.

After joining us for several miles, Jayne did a quick count of how many runners there would be arriving in Wells, before returning ahead of us to cook us all another amazing breakfast. These breakfasts proved a great source of fuel and lifted the whole team's morale. It also gave me enough time to have my feet redressed.

On arriving home I felt so relieved to have completed another circuit. I had now covered 296 miles with only another 112 miles to go until I could reach the world record.

At 2:32pm on Saturday, after peeling off each sock along with another layer of tattered skin, I managed a long shower and then re-dressed my broken feet. It was time to start running the fifth circuit. I resisted the temptation for a quick sleep as I had very little time to get ready before my support car arrived.

The hills into Bath proved really demanding and took their toll on my tired legs, which needed assistance once more from my equally exhausted arms.

I really felt I needed some sleep at this stage, but refused point blank to give in, until I had at least cleared the city of Bath and was well on my way into Bristol.

Heading out from Bath along a busy dual-carriageway, I was convinced that I had dropped my jacket and went to pick it up from the grass verge – only to be told by my support runner that it wasn't my jacket, but a discarded bin liner! We both stopped and looked at each other for a moment, before bursting out laughing – sleep deprivation was certainly taking its toll! I continued running and quickly changed the conversation in embarrassment, hoping they would soon forget my error!

At midnight, while running through the busy streets of Bristol with the flag flying high above my backpack, we were approached by several groups of people all enjoying a Saturday night out on the town. It took a while longer than usual to leave the centre as people wanted to have photos taken with us. Generous donations were also made, along with kind gestures such as "good luck" and "keep going, you can do this".

Arriving at the suspension bridge at 2:20am I had a quick break and several mugs of coffee to try and keep me awake, before agreeing to meet the support car a couple of miles further on outside Bristol City Football Club's stadium, Ashton Gate.

On arriving at the deserted road that led to the football ground, we could see the support car parked about 200 metres ahead of us. The driver had given a lift to one of my support runners who had been running for hours with me and now needed to rest before returning back to her car. With them in our sights, we suddenly saw a blinding array of flashing blue lights pull up behind them. On approaching, we saw two policemen emerge from their vehicle and ask what they were doing there. The look on the poor driver's face as we passed was a picture! All we could hear was "that's the fellow there, that's him". As he frantically tried to explain to the officers why he was parked up at 3am on the side of a deserted road with a young lady in his brand new Mercedes.

Luckily the officers had heard about my run on the TV and allowed them to carry on with my support. On passing they gave us a blue light salute and wished us a safe journey. Despite our pleas, they refused to lock the driver up for the night!

Refreshed from all the banter, we quickly ran to the top of Dundry Hill which seemed so much easier than the previous day.

Noticing that my feet were beginning to really hurt while descending from Dundry, I stopped to give them some attention.

On removing my trainers it quickly became apparent that both my socks had completely worn through on the bottoms, revealing bare feet to the mercy of my trainers! A big smile emerged on my support driver's face as I held up the bottomless socks for him to see. After quickly replacing the offending articles we were making good time, passing through narrow country lanes, listening to the incredible dawn chorus of birds enjoying the early morning sunshine.

With the sunrise now reflecting a golden glow from the still surface of Chew Valley Lake, it was a complete contrast to the previous days' view, when I had passed at 3am.

At the lake I was met by a couple of new support runners who had kindly brought out a flask of porridge for my breakfast. Feeling so tired I decided to quickly snatch a short power nap and have the meal afterwards. Ten minutes later I woke to find the ladies frantically shaking the flask to try and release the porridge from within, much to the amusement of the driver. What came out tasted really good though.

The sun had remained out all morning which soon dried out all the lanes and made running conditions far less of a challenge than before.

On approaching Wells Cathedral, I was jokingly told that the 6th Rifles Division were playing in the grounds to welcome me. On arriving we found out that they were there to celebrate the unveiling of a statue of the late, great, First World War veteran Harry Patch who lived in the city. As we entered the grounds, we were approached by both the BBC and ITV news teams who had just finished filming the event, and asked if we could give a quick interview for the evening news.

Despite losing time, I was grateful to have the TV companies raise awareness for both the CHSW charity and our record-breaking attempt.

One part of the circuit involved a steady five-and-a-half-mile climb, which always proved very monotonous. On this particular occasion it was my fifth attempt and I was starting to feel the side-effects of lack of sleep. Stubbornly, I continued on in autopilot mode, which was fine when I was running on a long straight section of footpath, but when the pavement went around a sharp corner I ran straight on and plummeted head first into a bramble hedge! My support runners just stood there in a shocked state of disbelief until I burst out laughing, before they all joined in.

Missing several of my planned breaks in order to make up for lost time, I soon reached the welcome but brief comfort of home. It had been the best finish to any of the previous circuits that I had run that week, and the weather had made such a difference, along with the fantastic support of the crews.

The time was now 7:40pm and this would be my last stop at home before a full day's run would soon follow. I had covered 370 miles with only 39 more to complete until reaching the world record target.

Quickly I showered, in the luxury of my simple bathroom, which felt like heaven as I relieved my aches and pains. Reluctantly, I changed into fresh kit and knew I had to desperately refocus in order to stay positive and complete the task ahead.

As I drank endless cups of tea from the huge teapot, my thoughts concentrated on the CHSW charity and all the incredible support from local running clubs and everyone who knew me. I wasn't going to let anybody down at this stage. It didn't matter how much I hurt or how bad my feet were, I was now only a day away from the record. After this I could rest or even retire from ultra-distance running and concentrate on half or full marathon distances instead.

A knock on my door took me instantly away from my thoughts, as the next support crew had arrived to load their car for the next 13 hours of support.

Quickly fitting my trainers, I picked up the day's running schedule and set off at 9:20pm to compete the sixth and final circuit.

It was indescribable how much my poor feet now hurt. During

the short time I had been at home they had settled and began to recover slightly. Sores and large cracks had temporarily bonded back together, but now I was on the move again all that had been forced apart with each and every painful step.

All I could focus on was the fact that, after today, I would only have to run the ten miles back into Bath again one more time and that would be it, I could finish in front of Bath Abbey and relax.

With support runners at my side, we arrived in the deserted streets of Bath at midnight. The city looked so beautiful with its dimly-lit cobbled streets. Landmarks like the Abbey, Circus and Royal Crescent were, once again, great distractions as I passed each one under the soft glow of night.

By 4:30am I had reached the centre of Bristol and felt really uncomfortable with my sore feet. I tried to change my socks but they had completely stuck to my feet and proved too painful to remove. With the dressing unable to do its job properly due to the constant impact of the roads and pavements, I made the decision to add a thinner pair of socks over the existing ones before carrying on.

I was now only 16 miles away from the record and still had 27-and-a-half hours in which to continue running. But my main concern was causing permanent damage to my feet and the risk of serious infection getting into them.

After leaving Bristol, the sun began to slowly rise as I made the final ascent of Dundry Hill. Rewarding myself with the breathtaking views I tried to distract myself from the painful descent. I constantly tried to stay positive by thinking that this was the last time I would have to run through each location.

Each mile now taken felt so much nearer to achieving a new record. I kept repeating this thought to myself, time and time again, as I soon realised I had reached Chew Valley Lake and the 400-mile mark. This brought me so much relief and distraction from all the aches and pains. It felt at one stage an impossible barrier to ever reach, but now I had crossed it and had only nine miles to go.

As I took one final glance at the lake behind me, the sky suddenly opened once more releasing a huge torrential downpour of rain. Within no time at all the roads and lanes were quickly flooded once again, which really began to worry me regarding my wet feet and the high risk of infection. Gradually the rain began to ease and was replaced with a misty haze that engulfed the whole of the Chew Valley region.

On reaching East Harptree, I saw through the mist a big group of runners all cheering and patiently waiting to join me on the final four miles to reach my target of 409 miles.

Quickly I devoured handfuls of snacks along with several cups of tea. All I had to do now was stay focused and enjoy the fantastic atmosphere that radiated from all my amazing support team.

Through flooded lanes we charged on relentlessly, enjoying a huge positivity amongst us all. Wiping the rain from our faces and occasionally shaking the excess moisture from our hair, we slowly but surely covered each mile with a sense of excitement. After making the ascent to reach Emborough Church, which stands proudly overlooking the valleys surrounding Chewton Mendip, we ran along the main road that led to the Old Down Inn in Emborough.

Trying to avoid the huge puddles and all the spray coming from passing traffic, I looked up to see the BBC news team waiting ahead in the pouring rain. They were equipped with all their gear to film us breaking the current world record live as it happened.

I couldn't believe it as I passed the 409-mile marker placed on the roadside for all to see, just outside the Old Down Inn. I had covered the distance with just under 21 hours to spare!

I was greeted by an ecstatic crowd of well-wishers, friends, family and fellow runners, then given a great interview by the BBC and reunited for a while with my dog Paddo, who had been brought along to join in the celebrations.

After doing an interview for the BBC and several other radio stations, I managed to quickly refuel on snacks before carrying on to extend my mileage.

My first place to visit after leaving Emborough was Midsomer Norton Rugby Club, to run a circuit of all their pitches in remembrance of my two cousins, Steve and Phil, who had helped me so much during my illness. While running the circuit around the rugby fields upon which they'd had so much fun, I envisaged Phil's contagious smile and wondered what sarcastic comment he would have made this time!

After making my way several more miles I finally arrived to an incredible reception outside my home in Westfield. Friends and neighbours were out in force celebrating with banners, balloons and flags everywhere. To me the best part was seeing everyone together, both young and old, standing side by side, all celebrating what can be achieved if you truly believe in yourself.

After meeting and talking to everyone, I had a quick shower and change of kit, while struggling to remove my socks that were still firmly stuck to my feet. Adding another pair of socks to cover the existing ones, I tried to hide the situation from everyone and walk around as comfortably as possible to avoid attention.

At 2:10pm I left home complete with a huge contingent of support runners to guide me safely into Bath, for the final section of my mammoth run.

I felt so glad after covering the mile-long hill out of Radstock, knowing that tomorrow I wouldn't have to run it anymore. A reward was waiting for me at the top as a large group of supporters presented me with a huge pasty on a plate of beans, which disappeared in minutes!

Feeling so pleased with what I had accomplished, the rest of the run up over Dunkerton Hill seemed much easier than it had done all week. I now knew that I had only five more miles remaining until I finally finished.

I could have finished earlier, but I knew that I wouldn't be satisfied until I had pushed the mileage even further and completed the hard run back into Bath.

At the top of Dunkerton Hill, I had my final short break and thanked the 16 support runners who were with me. Two of them were children, Gertie and Oscar, along with their patents, Dan and Claire, who had ran so many miles on this event with me.

This was it now, the final push into Bath and no more stops until I reached the magnificent Abbey. As I looked back over my shoulder, I felt so proud to see all the support I had as I ran into the city – even Paddo was stood up anxiously on the passenger seat of the support car.

We all recieved an amazing reception from passing motorists and the general public who recognised us from all the media coverage. Crowds gave us plenty of room as we ran up through the final few hundred metres of Southgate shopping centre, before finally turning right into Abbey churchyard. With the huge Abbey now standing magnificently before us, the adrenalin fuelled my body as I managed to sprint up to the doors before leaning into them. I turned around to face a courtyard of spectators going crazy before me.

A huge bottle of champagne was presented to me, which I quickly opened with a stream of bubbles as the cork disappeared over the heads of the excited onlookers.

As I drank the champagne from the bottle with one hand and held Paddo firmly clenched in the other, I found it hard to comprehend that I had actually achieved and finished this incredible event.

I had planned this event for six months and, at the age of 50, along with the outstanding support, managed to smash the existing record by running 426 miles in 6 days, 8 hours and 10 minutes – with another 15 hours and 50 minutes to spare. During that week, after adding up all the short power naps entered into the support driver's ledger, I had a total of just six hours sleep, burnt an estimated 50,000 calories and ran over 16 marathons back to back.

Immediately I was bombarded with non-stop radio interviews, which gave me the perfect opportunity to thank everyone for all their amazing support. Passing round the bottle of champagne to all the support crew and runners, I realised that Paddo was now sound asleep on my arm, despite all the excitement going on around us.

For about two hours I slowly walked around and mingled with the crowds, not daring – despite many suggestions that I should – to sit down, for the fear of not being able to stand up again.

When it was finally time to leave, I walked down to the car park trying to ignore and disguise all the tiredness and discomfort that I felt. Under all the smiles of jubilation that I portrayed I really hurt, but wouldn't let it show as I didn't like to show any signs of weakness.

Some friends kindly drove me and Paddo back home to Westfield, where I really struggled with getting out of the car. I got showered and changed, then for the first time in 24 hours, checked how bad a state my feet were in. As I removed my socks, which I had to wear in the shower in order to soak and release them, large patches of skin came off to expose raw nerves and exposed skin. Carefully, after applying antiseptic cream and fresh socks, I emerged with a slight hobble, huge smile, redressed and ready to go to the pub to celebrate with everyone.

At the local pub it felt so good to finally sit down and relax; now I could enjoy a roast dinner along with a few pints of refreshing Guinness to celebrate.

At the end of the evening, after returning home, it felt really good to relax with my three dogs snuggled around me, just knowing that I didn't have to go out and run another 74-mile circuit in all weathers.

As I sat for a few brief moments, I just smiled as I looked around my home. On the dining table were all the laminated schedules that I had carried from day to day. Next to them was a huge basket full of used running kit that had accumulated throughout the week. Then next to that was a tired looking Union Jack that now hung motionless for the first time in a week. It was still attached to a filthy looking backpack that had endured so much bad weather and spray off the roads from passing vehicles. But best of all, as I unzipped the backpack, I found a fluffy bear still with a smile on his face and wearing the CHSW neckerchief, which had been with me throughout the whole event. The idea behind me carrying this little friend was that he could be later auctioned off to raise funding for the Children's Hospice.

With the washing machine now doing overtime and my poor feet soaking in a really hot bowl of salted water, I sat and contemplated what I would be doing next as a fund-raising event. Quickly, I came to the conclusion that I should now retire from ultra-running, as I knew that I couldn't push my body any harder than I had done that week. I had experienced pain like never before and unimaginable bouts of sleep deprivation which had tormented and stretched me to extreme limits.

Through all the smiles, I had kept going, but knew deep inside that this was now enough, it was time to enjoy other sporting events. I could go back to free-lung diving from my kayak off the shores of Lulworth Cove, or catch some large waves surfing off the beautiful coastline of Cornwall, or the Bay of Biscay in France.

Carefully I patted my feet dry and redressed them before going out on a painful three mile jog with the dogs. I really didn't want to, but knew if I didn't I could face serious organ failure, after pushing my body to its limits for over a week. Every six hours, I would repeat the same exercise for the following two days.

Despite being absolutely exhausted, I couldn't sleep for any more than a couple of hours at a time. I would suddenly wake up thinking that I was still out there running.

It was amazing that in just a few days my feet began to repair and heal themselves. My extra couple of days holiday that I had booked from work had now passed and soon I was absorbed once again in my day to day responsibilities. But in just eight days time I would be carrying the Olympic Torch through Frome High Street.

THE OLYMPIC DREAM

Returning home from work one evening, I found that my London Olympics uniform had arrived. Nervously I didn't open the package until I had showered and polished the dining room table to open it on. To my surprise it contained a short letter stating that due to an extremely high demand for the large size they were only able to provide me with an X-large size instead!

When I tried on the trousers, I could have nearly put two people inside, and the same applied to the top. I was now getting extremely anxious, as thoughts raced through my mind of my trousers falling down around my ankles, as I held the Olympic torch high above me while running through Frome High Street!

Desperately looking for a way to make the outfit secure, I found a drawstring in the waistline of the trousers that I could tighten up a good four inches higher than my belly button!

After several practise sessions in front of Paddo, I found this hid my huge waistline and held my legs high enough not to cover my new trainers and drag along the floor.

With the top, I learnt to roll up the sleeves and use a secret elastic band to hold them up out of the way – otherwise they would have been well over the length of my hands and I would have looked a right mess!

At 7pm on 21st May, I was invited to a civic reception in recognition of the Bath & North East Somerset Olympic Torch Bearers at the Roman Baths.

With burnt fingers after several attempts to iron my shirt properly, I was greeted by the Chairman of Bath & North East Somerset Council, along with 26 other torch bearers, to celebrate the passing of the Olympic flame through our area while on its journey to London.

It was really good to meet the other torch bearers and hear how they felt about carrying the Olympic flame in front of so many people in less than 24 hours time. It came as a great relief to find that most of them were as nervous as I was.

Just before the evening drew to a close, I was presented with a special blue engraved vase to represent my participation in the torch relay on 22nd May.

Everything was suddenly feeling real now and the enormity of the event started to make me really proud and extremely nervous. Several times during the night, I would wake up and go through all the instructions in my mind. Despite me taking the day off work I still got up at 5am as usual to have breakfast and prepare for the exciting day ahead.

Arriving early at my collection point at Frome Community College, I read through my instructions time and time again. Here I met the members of the London Organising Committee before getting changed into my uniform and boarding the shuttle bus that would take us all to our allocated starting places. In the front of the bus was a large stand that held all the Olympic torches immaculately on display. Each one labelled with our individual number, so that we all had our own torch to carry and be presented with to take home afterwards.

As the shuttle bus left the college with all the participants the streets of Frome were beginning to fill with spectators for the big event.

With clear skies and bright sunshine, it was a magnificent day for everyone. As the sun's rays entered through the shuttle bus windows it reflected off all the golden torches, sending a cascade of sparkling reflections that filled the inside of the vehicle, adding to the magical atmosphere of the event.

With the shuttle bus now ready to drop the first torch bearer in position just before noon, we were all ready to take on our responsibilities alongside the security staff that accompanied the

Olympic flame throughout its journey.

As we approached the main streets of Frome, it was incredible how many people had come along to watch. Earlier there were only a few lining the streets, now they lined the entire length of Frome, filling every pavement and balcony available.

I was the fourth torch bearer to be dropped at my designated spot, which involved running 300 metres along the main High Street.

While I stood there waiting for the previous bearer to appear, I could hardly hear what the security team were saying due to all the noise. Surrounded by tall buildings full of people looking out of their windows and standing in every available space, the whole atmosphere was truly incredible.

Countless people would stand next to me to have their photographs taken; at one point I suddenly found a three-week-old baby in my empty left arm as I held the torch high with my right one! I just prayed that the mother would reclaim the little one before I had to set off down the road.

I now felt really nervous and remembered how I had tied the drawstring of my trousers four times, in case it decided to have a mind of its own. Endless thoughts raced through my mind as the security staff primed the gas cylinder in my torch: don't go out on me, don't trip or fall over, if you feel your trousers starting to fall remember you do have a spare left hand to rescue them!

I could now see the previous torch bearer approaching. The baby had been reclaimed and the security team did their job keeping the crowds at bay as they surrounded me in the middle of the road.

With the torch now held high in my right hand at a 45-degree angle, the previous runner gently passed the precious Olympic flame onto my torch. This was referred to in my instruction book as the 'Olympic Kiss'.

With my torch now supporting the strong Olympic flame, I was given the all clear to start my run down through the Market Place.

I couldn't help but look up at the flame that engulfed the top of my torch, which filled me with an incredible sense of pride. Focusing back on where I was going, and surrounded by a large security team, I ran into the most intense atmosphere of the crowds.

Never in my life had I ever experienced such enthusiasm as that day. The whole situation felt unreal and it was an absolute honour for me to represent the local community. To have the Olympic games going ahead in Britain and here above me, being held in my hand, was the actual flame that has travelled 8,000 miles, all the way from the ancient Temple of Hera in Olympia, to eventually light the Olympic games in London.

Throughout the incredible experience, I would occasionally hear an extra loud scream or shout that caught my attention from people that I knew, hidden in the depths of the jubilant crowds.

As I looked casually from side to side and then back up at the flame, just to check and reassure myself that everything was okay, the security team would smile back as if to say, "you aren't the first person we've seen do that", then discreetly give me the thumbs up to keep me calm.

I was now on the final 50 metres of my run, tackling a steep hill, where I could see a young lady ahead holding her torch high up ready to receive the Olympic flame.

Closely watched by the security team, we exchanged the flame in true style – the only thing it didn't mention in the instruction book was how your whole arm would be shaking with excitement. I watched as the lady continued up the hill and out of sight amongst all the onlookers. The noise and atmosphere as the flame was exchanged was absolutely amazing – a memory that will last me a lifetime.

Quickly surrounded by another security team, I was guided aboard the shuttle bus as another member of the team removed the gas cylinder from my torch, placing a special label on it before returning it to the standard holder that was guarded by even more security.

Slowly as we followed the Olympic entourage through the rest of Frome, we picked up all the torch bearers and waved back at the ecstatic crowds as they continued to support us on our incredible journey. The shuttle bus then made its way back to the college where we were each presented with the Olympic torch that we had carried. This I will treasure forever – little did I know at the time, how much proud work I'd be doing with it in the years to come.

The month of May had been an unbelievable one. First of all taking the current world record and then, just two weeks later, carrying the Olympic flame.

Just days after breaking the record, I was receiving emails, letters and phone calls asking me if I would like to open sports days at several schools, attend village fetes and country shows as well as giving talks to various establishments.

My first attendance was opening the Cossington Country Fayre and music festival along with BBC Somerset presenter Emma Britton. This was my first time attending anything like this and I soon found all signs of nervousness disappear as I enjoyed taking part and meeting people. I would never have guessed eight years ago, while learning to walk again, that anything like this would ever happen to me. If it had back then I would have been so shy and reserved that I couldn't have taken part!

On Saturday 23rd June, I had a trail run booked as part of the 10-stage Cotswold Way relay that starts in Evesham and finishes in Bath. My running slot was the first stage, starting at 7:30am. In order to get there on time I had to drive from Westfield to Chipping Campden at 5am. Then park, get changed into my running gear and race for 12 miles, following the Cotswold Way path to finish at Stanway House.

After the run I managed to get a lift back to Chipping Campden, before driving 88 miles back home again. Once at home, I immediately got showered and changed into some smart clothes before driving a further five miles to arrive at Chewton Mendip, where I had the honour of opening their village fayre.

It was a really sunny afternoon as I showed all the children and their parents the Olympic Torch, before joining in with their sporting activities and country dancing.

Later in the afternoon I was invited to the top of Chewton Mendip church tower to look down on the surrounding fields where the fayre was being held. Taking the torch along with me, in the bright sunlight, I even managed to reflect golden rays of light from the tower down to the commentator below.

Immediately he announced over the PA system, "If everyone would care to look up at the church tower, you will see the golden reflection coming from John's Olympic Torch."

My next appearance with the torch was on 14th July in Wells where Mary Rand was given the 'freedom of the city'. It was to celebrate her winning a Gold medal back in 1964 when she won the long-jump in the Tokyo Olympic games, jumping a massive 6.72 metres. She later went on to win a Silver in Pentathlon and Bronze in the 4 x 100m relay at the same games, before returning to Wells for a hero's welcome.

This was an extra special occasion for me as I can vividly remember my mother taking me to Wells market place when I was very young to see the plaque that the city had made for Mary in the pavement, which spanned the 6.72 metre distance she had jumped. As I stood at one end and looked in sheer amazement at the distance, I couldn't believe that it was humanly possible to achieve – it took me long enough at the age of five to walk it!

Every time I ran through Wells on my ultra-distance events, I would pass it and special memories would come flooding back to me. Never had I imagined that I would get to meet Mary, and have the chance to hold all her priceless medals in my hands and talk to her about her sporting achievements.

I met Mary as she presented a series of awards to the Wells

City Harriers' leading junior athletes. I had been asked by the club's chairman to wear my torch bearer's uniform and have several photographs taken with her. She was very interested in how I managed to run the 426 miles in just over six days and then explained to me all about the training she used to do in order to achieve her amazing goals at the Olympic games.

Mary freely passed around all her medals for the youngsters to see and the look on all their faces was absolutely priceless. They had been inspired to dream that, maybe one day, they might be able to win medals of their own.

Over the following months, I ran relatively short distances with the local running clubs. I concentrated more on speed, over short trail runs, and trained others for their first, half or full marathons. Any thoughts of running extreme-ultras simply didn't exist now, as my spare time was taken up with giving talks to various groups.

By booking more holiday off from work, I was able to attend a lot of the local schools and give talks about the positivity and adventures that can be gained through sport.

Bringing the Olympic Torch along to events also proved very popular and I had a job to keep up with all the bookings. I never charged for my time as I was just glad to see the reaction from the audience, showing others what could be achieved.

Later in August, I received a letter from CHSW inviting me to attend a presentation at the Charlton Farm hospice in Wraxall to celebrate my efforts in raising £50,000 for the charity. It was a really emotional moment when I received a special piece of artwork created by the children and siblings visiting the hospice. This was presented by the youngsters themselves on a sunny afternoon, in the full beauty of the gardens filled with the scent of the fragrant flowers.

As I received my gift, all the thoughts of my amazing adventures came flooding back, the first 110-mile run between the two hospices, along with endless hours of running to achieve 140, 300 and, finally, the 426-mile record.

All my inspiration had come from the strength and determination of the children and their families that I had met while receiving support from the CHSW care teams. Along with all the fundraising and media awareness for CHSW, I also calculated that I had helped raise over £10,000 for several other charities during my eight years of running events.

Later that evening after the presentation, I made my excuses to the local running group that I wouldn't be able to attend. I knew that I now needed some time to reflect back on just what had happened over the past eight years, and more importantly, where was I going to go from here!

Sitting quietly at home with Paddo asleep on my lap and my springers, Scooby and Bonnie, resting on my feet, it felt really good for once to have time to myself. The dogs must have thought it was a real luxury as I very rarely gave myself any spare time. I was either working, planning the next big event, giving talks and presentations or out training others at my Westfield running group.

In a peculiar way, it felt strange to have my own time and not feel guilty about relaxing but actually enjoy it. I wouldn't switch on the TV as I just loved to sit and think things through without being disturbed or distracted.

Reflecting back on how my running had started purely by chance in 2004 and, ironically, how much I actually hated it – especially after completing my first half marathon – I found myself smiling down at Paddo, who just seemed to understand my every thought. I then realised that I had tears running down the side of my face as precious memories of my late cousins, Steve and Phil, came flooding back. The agony of how much I missed their company and especially all the banter always hit me hard. Often, I would wonder what they would say if they saw how far their influence had driven me.

Paddo, now with his paws resting firmly on each of my shoulders, quickly mopped away any remaining salty tears and brought a smile back to my face. He was always there for me and seemed to understand every emotion I had.

Previously, after each long run that I did, I always had another planned – sometimes before the previous one had even been completed. But this time I had nothing and seemed to know my limitations, which for now I was completely satisfied with.

My running distances were now relatively short compared to what I had been doing. But they were a lot quicker and seemed to control the problem of the seizures that I so regularly experienced at night, whenever I rested.

As the darkness of the evening slowly began to fill the living room, I decided to light the wood burner for an hour, just to take the chill out of the house. I didn't bother to switch on any lighting, as I loved to sit with Paddo and watch the mesmerising patterns coming from the flames as they consumed the logs within. From out of the corner of my eye, I could see the reflection of the cosy fire shining off my Olympic Torch, which stood proudly polished in its stand. All the memories of that great day back in May came flooding back along with all the countless appearances I had made with it since.

Although I had experienced a great family loss of two of the closest people to me, suffered no end of pain just accomplishing everyday chores, then pushed myself through horrendous mental and physical barriers, I was still here!

I had been so lucky to experience all the incredible adventures, and still find it hard to believe that they had happened to me. All this had been made possible by the amazing people around me, who supported and believed in me, and formed an incredible team to make the impossible, possible.

For now, I could just sit peacefully, feeling relaxed and proud, having finally banished my demon and replaced it with an angel on my shoulder.

What I had accomplished so far had been phenomenal, but little did I know what might lay ahead of me.

Children's Hospice South West (CHSW)

Children's Hospice South West (CHSW) was first registered with the charity commission in 1991 and is dedicated to making the most of short and precious lives, providing the best possible hospice care for children and young people with life-limiting conditions and their families.

The charity provides specialist palliative care, resilience stays for the whole family, a sibling service for brothers and sisters, emergency support, end of life care and a bereavement service for as long as is needed.

Its three hospices Charlton Farm in Wraxall, North Somerset, Little Bridge House in North Devon, and Little Harbour in Cornwall ensure that no family is more than 90 minutes from a local children's hospice when care is needed most.

Charlton Farm opened in 2007 to provide care for families in Somerset and the surrounding area. The hospice now looks after more than 230 children with life limiting illnesses thanks to the amazing fundraising of supporters like John.

Over the years, John has taken on so many challenges in support of CHSW, including half marathons, full marathons, ultra-marathons and extreme marathons. He has inspired so many people with these challenges and the charity was thrilled that John was chosen to run with the Olympic torch through Frome in recognition of his fundraising.

CHSW is continuing to support families now and for many years to come from the good times and the magical times, to the hard times and goodbye times, together the charity can make the most of short and precious lives.

To find out more about the ways that you can support CHSW and to read more about how your kindness makes a difference to families, visit www.chsw.org.uk